A BRIEF
INTRODUCTION
TO SPEECH

A BRIEF INTRODUCTION TO SPEECH

Donovan J. Ochs

The University of Iowa

Anthony C. Winkler

 HARCOURT BRACE JOVANOVICH, INC.
New York / San Diego / Chicago / San Francisco / Atlanta

ISBN: 0-15-505583-6

Library of Congress Catalog Card Number: 78-73850

Printed in the United States of America

Page 223, listing copyrights and acknowledgments,
constitutes a continuation of the copyright page.

PREFACE

We wrote this book for students who want to speak effectively to an audience. We believe that students do not come into a speech course unable to communicate. Indeed, college students have had considerable experience in the various ways of communicating—talking, reading, listening, and writing. They already have many of the skills needed for some type of clear, purposeful communication. By pointing out the similarities and differences between talking and *presenting a speech*, between writing and *speaking*, between reading and *doing research for a speech*, we show students how to use the skills they already have and what new skills they must acquire in order to present an effective speech.

The chapters in Part 2 organize the speechmaking task: choosing a topic and finding the central idea; using supporting details; gathering materials; making an outline; constructing and wording the speech; practicing speech delivery. A novel feature of this text is that it focuses on the oral paragraph as the basic module of a speech. Building on the students' familiarity with written paragraphs, the text emphasizes how the skills acquired in writing paragraphs may be successfully adapted to constructing oral paragraphs.

The chapters on listening, speechfright, and revising the speech should help students to understand that speaking is a process, not an isolated experience. What we believe we have accomplished is to present the speech process in a form, in a tone of voice, that allows students to actually give speeches instead of just reading about them.

Speaking effectively to an audience is a skill. It is a skill that can be acquired and then developed. We have tried to provide, within a brief compass, a guide to mastering this skill.

Donovan J. Ochs

Anthony C. Winkler

CONTENTS

Listening   13

Coping with Speechfright   31

PART   SPEECH
PREPARATION
AND
DELIVERY   45

The Topic and the Central Idea   47

How to Use Supporting Details   61

Gathering Materials 79

Making an Outline 101

Constructing Oral Paragraphs   115

Wording the Speech   137

Practicing Speech Delivery   157

Revising the Speech   167

PART

GENERAL TYPES OF SPEECHES   173

The Speech to Inform   175

The Speech to Persuade   199

Topical Table of Contents:
Answers to Student Questions About Speech

A BRIEF
INTRODUCTION
TO SPEECH

1

SPEAKERS
AND
LISTENERS

1

Using your speech skills

My voice goes after what my eyes cannot reach.
—Walt Whitman

DEFINITION OF COMMUNICATION

The word "communicate" is derived from the Latin *communicatus* meaning to share, to impart, to make common. And by the time you are able to read this book, you will have already done a great deal of communicating. You communicate daily with friends, loved ones, relatives, and strangers. You share your thoughts on the trivial and the significant: how you want your hamburger cooked; why you are leery of Scorpios; and what you would do if you were president. No accurate estimate exists on the number of words students typically use during the course of a single day, but common sense tells us that the sum is considerable. And all these words are used in the cause of *communicatus,* the goal being to share and impart your attitudes, feelings, wishes, and dreams to another person.

Understandably, therefore, speech teachers are mystified every semester when students swear that they will make fools of themselves if they ever try to give a speech, for these same students can usually be found talking energetically in the hallway or in the cafeteria. If you are capable of ordinary social conversation, with training and practice you can learn how to present a speech before an audience.

Personal conversation

In fact, many of the skills you use in private conversation are indistinguishable from the skills you use in a public speech. Consider, for instance, a simple conversation with someone. You say something; the person responds; you evaluate their response and make a reply. If you become conscious of boring or displeasing the person, you probably change the subject. And under ordinary circumstances, the other person would do the same for you. Moreover, during the course of this exchange, you automatically adjust your vocabulary, syntax, and message, depending on the person you are talking to. For instance, if the other person is a close friend, you might address him or her using slang and a good deal of light banter. You might open the conversation by saying, "What's going on?" or "What's happening?" But it is highly unlikely that you would take the same tone, send the same message, use the same words, if the other person were a graying senior professor, your dignified and austere great-grandmother, or the avuncular family physician who delivered you into this world. Only infants determinedly babble the same message, no matter who is listening. Under ordinary circumstances, most of us adjust our conversation to fit the situation we are in and the person to whom we are talking.

Public speaking

If you were giving a speech before an audience, you would make similar adjustments, but with more premeditation. You would take into account the audience you intend to address, selecting a subject you think would appeal to them, as well as expressing it in language you think they would understand. If your audience became restless during the course of the speech, you would realize that you were boring them and adjust your presentation accordingly. In sum, giving a speech is not an act exotically different from talking to another person.

There are, however, some differences between the two, which we must consider. First, a speaker cannot address an audience in the same soft tone of voice that could be used when speaking to a single person. Some intensification of voice and mannerisms is necessary if a speaker wishes to assert his or her presence before an audience. The speaker must use visible and conspicious gestures, a loud voice, and generally employ an emphatic and heightened delivery in order to be seen, heard, and understood.

Second, complex ideas are more readily explained and more easily understood in a one-to-one talk than in a formal public speech. Speechmaking involves the one communicating to the many; the more minds involved, the greater the chance of misunderstanding. Speakers, therefore, do not ordinarily try to explain abstract or complex notions. Subtleties, faint shades of meaning, and ambiguities do not generally fare well in speeches. Instead, speeches are usually structured and developed around one or two primary ideas that are carefully stated, restated, and exemplified.

In sum, formal speechmaking is to personal conversation what the breast stroke is to the back stroke. Both strokes are variants of swimming; both speechmaking and casual talking are forms of communication. The swimmer who knows how to swim one stroke can readily learn the other. Likewise, the student who has spent a lifetime talking, can learn to give formal speeches.

The best place to acquire and refine the skills necessary for making formal speeches is in the classroom. The student who does poorly at giving a single in-class speech knows that, at worst, only the grade will suffer. Neither job, prestige, nor reputation are at stake as they would be in the outside world. It's not as though one had just badly flubbed a presentation at a sales meeting, drawing a severe frown from the sales manager, with the promise of a later "chewing out" or even a pink slip. An audience of fellow students is likely to be sympathetic towards the fumbling, nervous beginning speaker, since everyone in the class is in the same boat. There is hardly a better sounding board against which one can safely practice and improve one's skill at public speaking. Students can coach one another, criticize one another, and applaud one another, without fear of doing themselves either economic harm or social injury.

SPEAKING AND WRITING: SOME DIFFERENCES

That a good writer is necessarily a good speaker is surely one of the most common fallacies. Writing and speaking are as little alike as stone and water. The written word exists on paper; a speech exists in utterance. Consequently, the difference between writing and speaking—from an audience's point of view—is really the difference between reading and listening. A reader sees; a listener hears. Plainly,

this must make for a difference between the language styles of writing and speaking. The reader sees the writer's words but cannot hear
the writer's voice; the listener hears the speaker's voice, but cannot
see the speaker's words. The reader has the advantage of instant
replay of every word and sentence on the page. Listeners must either
ask speakers to repeat themselves, or must depend on their memory
of what was said.

The language of a speech must necessarily be more repetitious
than the language of writing. Consider, for instance, the following
passage:

> We shall defend our island, whatever the cost may be. We shall
> fight on the beaches. We shall fight on the landing grounds. We
> shall fight in the fields and in the streets, and we shall fight in
> the hills. We shall never surrender.

The passage is taken from a speech made by Winston Churchill after
the withdrawal of British troops from Dunkirk. A writer would have
probably put it this way:

> We shall defend our island—at whatever cost—by fighting on the
> beaches and the landing grounds, in the fields, streets, and hills.
> But we shall never surrender.

The extract now boasts a more complex sentence structure, complete
with a parenthetical clause. This is the sort of expression that fares
well on the page. But the passage has lost its wonderful exhortative
quality resulting from the repetition.

In addition, the language of a speech tends to be more colloquial
than the language of writing. There is something about the petrifica-
tion of print that demands the utmost in grammar and exactness. In
a speech, grammatical niceties give way to informality and colloquialisms, and the speaker who insists on being excessively grammatical and formal often ends up seeming merely rigid and pedantic.
Consider, for instance, this brief excerpt from a famous speech by
Sojourner Truth, an American abolitionist:

> The man over there says women need to be helped into car-
> riages, and lifted over ditches, and to have the best place every-

> where. Nobody ever helps me into carriages or over puddles, or gives me the best place—and ain't I a woman?
>
> I could work as much and eat as much as a man—when I could get it—and bear the lash as well! And ain't I a woman?

Part of the intensity of the speech is derived from its colloquial phrasing. "Aren't I a woman?" or "Am I not a woman?" although more formally correct than "Ain't I a woman?" nevertheless lack the force and impact of the original.

Finally, speeches tend to amplify and restate ideas over and over again, to make them more easily and better understood by an audience. The starkness of words on a page makes this sort of amplification neither necessary nor desirable in writing. Examine this excerpt from Barry Goldwater's nomination acceptance speech, delivered at the Republican National Convention in 1964:

> This nation and its people are freedom's model in a searching world. We can be freedom's missionaries in a doubting world. But first *we must renew* freedom's vision in our hearts and in our homes.
>
> During four futile years, the Administration which we shall replace has distorted and lost that vision.
>
> It has talked and talked and talked about the *words* of freedom. But it has failed and failed and failed in the *works* of freedom.
>
> Failures cement the wall of shame in Berlin. Failures blot the sands of shame at the Bay of Pigs. Failures mark the slow death of freedom in Laos. Failures infest the jungles of Vietnam. Failures haunt the houses of our once great alliances, and undermine the greatest bulwark ever erected by free nations—the NATO community.

The whole passage simply amplifies on a rather frail contention about freedom: Namely that we have it, others don't, but we are losing it. To make this point, the speaker expended some one-hundred-thirty words, cataloging example after example of how we are losing freedom. In print, this would have been excessively tedious and boring. The passage, however, fared considerably better as a speech, and worked its desired effect on the audience of delegates.

It follows from this discussion, that writing and speaking are different enough as forms of expression to require students to practice both diligently. The good writer is not necessarily a good speaker, nor the good speaker necessarily a good writer. Nor, for that matter, will the techniques that work for writing necessarily transfer successfully to speaking. Some do and some don't. (For similarities between writing and speaking see Chapter 9.) Writers learn to write well and speakers learn to speak well through practice.

CHARACTERISTICS OF A SPEECH

All speeches are not created equal; some are long, some short, some boring, some exciting. They range in complexity from a lecture on theoretical physics presented at a meeting of scientists to a five-minute pep talk on courtesy given to a troop of cub scouts. Speeches vary in formality from an address to the General Assembly of the United Nations to a blitzkrieg spiel delivered at your doorstep by a determined peddler. Endless variations are to be expected in any form of communication that serves so many purposes and has so many uses. Yet, in spite of their variety, speeches have some elements in common—especially the kind of short speeches that college students are usually required to give. What are these shared characteristics?

Audience

This requirement is, as a lawyer might put it, the *sine qua non* (absolute requirement) of a speech. It is what distinguishes a speech from writing and what accounts for their differences in language styles. The written word exists primarily on paper; a speech exists in the utterance. Written words are premeditatedly put down on paper by a writer and bound over to drift down through the ages. A speech may or may not be written down beforehand, but it must be delivered by a speaker before an audience or it cannot technically be called a speech.

The giving of a speech is a unique, once-in-a-lifetime act because the elements that interact at the giving of any speech can never again be exactly the same. The *speaker* will never again be able to deliver the speech with exactly the same emphasis, tone, attention, and modulation with which he or she first gave it. The audience, even if made up of the same people who heard the speech before, cannot ever again exist in exactly the same condition.

Physical context   Speeches are also performed in a unique *physical context*. Moviemakers may use their magic to approximate the conditions of the historical past, but they cannot duplicate them. The chinks in the flooring that Lincoln may have occasionally gazed at while delivering his Second Inaugural Address have now gone the way of dry rot and dust. We do not know what the lighting was like during his Address, what the level of background noise was, nor how these things affected Lincoln. We have Lincoln's words left; but the physical context in which these words were spoken has been swallowed up.

Historical context   Neither can *historical context* be the same from one presentation of a speech to another since the events and circumstances that affect human life change. Moreover, the events of the moment provide a context in which the speaker's words appear intelligible and reasonable to an audience. The expression "neutron bomb" was, a year ago, meaningless to most Americans; today it is the subject of heated debate. Likewise, the speech by Franklin Delano Roosevelt, which began:

> Yesterday, December 7, 1941—a date which will live in infamy—the United States of America was suddenly and deliberately attacked by naval and air forces of the Empire of Japan.

and which declared war on Japan, has neither the significance nor the impact today that it had in its own unique historical context. Nor, for that matter, can it ever again.

In sum, the presentation of a speech is invested with all the singularity and significance that only a living act can have. After the speech is given, it exists on paper as a fossil.

Purpose

Speeches are given for three general purposes: to inform, to entertain, or to persuade. Hybrid combinations of these purposes are also possible. A speech, for instance, may both entertain and inform; likewise, it may also simultaneously inform and persuade.

Although each purpose may not exactly anticipate every conceivable reason that one might have for giving a speech, each is useful to the novice speaker. Teachers frequently assign speeches according to one of these purposes. Students might be asked to give a speech that informs, that entertains, or that persuades. With one of these general purposes in mind, student speakers have the distinct advantage of knowing approximately what they are expected to do, and are therefore less likely to be overwhelmed by the infinite. If the assignment calls for a speech to inform, the students know that they must gather data, information, and facts. If the assignment calls for a speech to entertain, students know that they must come up with a lighter topic, tone, and approach.

Central idea

All of us, at one time or another, have asked of a friend, relative, or colleague, "What's the big idea?"—an entirely appropriate query to direct at a speech. Lunatics might give speeches that have neither purpose nor meaning, but sane men and women are generally assumed to give a speech that has not only a purpose, but also a big idea.

The big idea of a speech—generally referred to as the "central idea"—is a statement of what the speech proposes to do. The speaker, for instance, who says "I want to talk to you today about the terrible effect inflation has on our pocket-books," has, in effect, announced the central idea of the speech. This announcement serves two functions: It orients listeners on what to expect, the expectation making it considerably easier for them to listen; it provides the speaker with a definite focus that will, it is hoped, spare him or her from straying from the topic.

Structure

The structure of a speech is the arrangement of its ideas, materials, and words into an obvious and coherent order. A speaker, for instance, might announce:

> The purpose of my speech today is to provide some background information on *Alice in Wonderland,* to briefly discuss the career of the book since its publication, and to show how it is still relevant to children today.

This statement not only informs the audience of the central idea of the speech, but also acquaints them with the speech's structure. First, the speech will give background information on *Alice in Wonderland;* then it will discuss the career of the book; and finally, it will demonstrate how the book is still relevant to children today. This obvious stacking of ideas into some sensible and discernible order is referred to as the structure of a speech.

A speech can be generally said to have a beginning, a middle, and an end—stages of the speech characterized as much by function as by sequence. The function of the beginning is to engage the listeners' interest and introduce the central idea. The middle serves to elaborate on the central idea and substantiate its claim with evidence; the end should propose solutions, make recommendations, or draw conclusions.

This sort of formal structuring, though it may sound forbidding, is not peculiar to public speeches. It can be found to a lesser extent even in a casual chat. The difference is one of degree, not of kind. You may not plan in advance what you intend to say to a friend at lunch, but neither are you likely to garble what you do say. Speakers plot out structure in advance because it is easier to give a prepared speech than to make one up on the spot. When it comes time for you to draft your own first speech, the experience of thousands of chats with friends should help you considerably with your speech's structure.

CHAPTER

Listening

Nobody ever listened himself out of a job.
—Grover Cleveland

SOME FACTS ABOUT LISTENING

According to the best available research, most of us are horribly inefficient listeners. Typically we understand only one-half of what we listen to; after two months, we can recall only one quarter. In case you're puzzled about the margin of possible misunderstanding in a 50 percent listening efficiency, here is a dramatized example. A politician makes a catchy campaign statement at an election-year rally: "What this country needs is a chicken in every pot and two cars in every garage"—a stirring message of sixteen words. An audience that understands only 50 percent of the statement—eight words—might conceivably hear: "This country needs a chicken in two cars." Two months later, the audience will remember only 25 percent of the message—perhaps recalling these four words, "This country is chicken." Garage, pot, car, and interrogative pronoun have been forgotten. With the average person having only a 50 percent listening efficiency, it is very nearly a wonder that any communication is possible or that any politician can get elected.

This revelation, however, will probably neither horrify nor astound most readers. After all, a great deal of our listening is devoted to trivial matters, small talk, or entertainment, and neither Kojak, Colombo, or casual acquaintances seem to say anything worth listening to or remembering. So what if we listen badly? How important can it be to listen well?

It is of overwhelming importance to listen well. Studies show that some 70 percent of every day is spent in verbal communication. Of this time, 9 percent is spent writing, 16 percent reading, 30 percent talking, and 45 percent listening.[1] Moreover, although listening is the major input for a lot of prattle and trivia, it is also a primary force in the formation of opinion. It has been estimated that 60 percent of the ideas that people have are drawn not from the print media but from media that rely heavily on efficient listening, such as radio and television.[2] One survey, conducted during a national election, revealed that the electorate received 27 percent of their information on the candidates and the issues from newspapers and magazines, and 58 percent from radio and television.[3] Thus, in addition to bearing the brunt of day-to-day communication, listening is also one of the primary skills used in the formation of political and general opinions.

Widespread reliance on a skill as inefficiently practiced as listening will inevitably cause misunderstanding and confusion, which, in turn, may lead to disaster. Husbands and wives will not hear each other; employees will not understand their employers, and vice versa; oral instructions will be badly carried out. The worst aircraft disaster in history, a collision between two jumbo jets in the Canary Islands that took the lives of over three hundred people, has been—in the main—attributed to faulty pilot listening.

The electorate that listens poorly is easy prey to every glib political huckster—sometimes with devastating results. According to an eyewitness, Hitler's rise to power was due, in part, to poor listening by the German electorate:

> It was clear to him (Hitler) that he could only win the attention of the mass by avoiding the usual terminology and working with new words and new conceptions. His train of thought was of such generally compelling nature that people of different political directions could agree with it. So during his first public appearance in Hamburg, he was able within a single hour, to persuade a suspicious and reserved audience to applaud, and this applause increased until it became, at the conclusion, an enthusiastic ovation. Later the most level-headed listeners declared that, though they were still against the speaker and his party, Hitler himself was obviously much more reasonable than they had imagined.[4]

Obviously, it is nearly child's play for a politician to dupe an electorate that understands only a half of what it hears and remembers only a quarter. Innumerable other evils can be laid at the doorstep of faulty listening but the point has been made: Listening is a vitally important skill.

Finally, the ability to listen well is an acquired, not an inherited, skill. It does not correlate significantly with intelligence. An intelligent person is not necessarily a good listener. Nor, for that matter, do people who listen a great deal automatically become better listeners. The contrary is more likely to be true: constant, though casual, listening tends to reinforce poor listening habits rather than eliminate them.

POOR LISTENING: CASE STUDY WITH COMMENTARY

The year is 1970; the Vietnam War is raging; student demonstrations are commonplace; the country is in a state of turmoil.

A young man named Harold is sitting in the placement office of his college. Harold graduated last month with a fairly decent GPA, and he desperately needs a job. But times are hard and few jobs are available. He has scrounged around looking for work, with no luck. Meanwhile, his dentist wants to be paid, his bank threatens to repossess his car, and his landlady vows to throw him out unless he pays the back rent. Harold is waiting to be interviewed by Mr. Speck, the sales manager of an office supply firm that is looking for a local representative.

The waiting room is dingy, noisy, and hot. There is a softball game going on behind the placement center and once in a while the room explodes with the rowdy shrieks of the players. Moreover, there is a pesky fly hovering in the room that occasionally swoops down to clean its feet on Harold's nose.

Harold has made himself as presentable as he can, given his impoverished state. He wears a white shirt and a colorful tie with a gaudy Hawaiian design—a gift from his mother. He has on a houndstooth sports coat that doesn't quite go with either the tie or the double-knit, flared pants—giving him an altogether too sporty look. He has shaved his beard for the interview, but he stubbornly holds on to a stylish fu-manchu mustache. His hair is cut just above the collar—not daringly long, but not Marine

Corps length either. Nevertheless, Harold thinks himself rather smartly dressed and waits with great expectations for the interviewer to arrive.

Half an hour later, the interviewer walks into the room. He is an older man, nearly sixty, who wears his hair in a spartan crewcut. He is immaculately dressed in a conservative business suit; his face is clean shaven; his lapels are adorned with two American flag pins. Mr. Speck and Harold look appraisingly at each other, shake hands, and sit down on opposite sides of a rickety table.

Mr. Speck reads Harold's application, clears his throat, looks at the young man sitting across from him, and asks: "I noticed it took you five years to get through school. Was there any special reason why you had to take an extra year?"

"I worked my way through by myself," Harold answers. "I couldn't take a full course load and keep my job at the same time."

Mr. Speck looks at Harold, taking in his collar-length hair, his sporty clothes, and his brazen fu-manchu mustache, and hears: "It took me five years to get through school because I was too busy partying and fooling around and protesting against everything to do much studying. Plus, I wanted to be sure the military didn't get me."

Commentary: People listen with their eyes

This proposition may startle at first, but on reflection will seem entirely reasonable. It is natural enough that an audience will use a speaker's dress and grooming to draw conclusions about the sort of person the speaker is. Mr. Speck, a conservative, middle-aged man, took one look at Harold's long hair, rakish mustache, and sporty dress, and saw before him an unrepentant radical who now wanted to make a living from the very system he had spent his college years denouncing.

This impulse, which we more or less all share, of appraising a speaker according to whether or not we like his looks has very ancient origins. Diogenes, the Greek philosopher, was ridiculed because he went about dressed in rags and tatters. Stories are legendary about innumerable prophets who were dismissed as mad or eccentric because they dressed differently than the people around them.

But listening with our eyes is a costly error in listening efficiency. If we are turned off by a speaker's dress or grooming, chances are we will block out what he has to say. We will hear, but not listen. Hearing refers simply to the stimulation of the auditory nerves by sound waves. We hear a bird sing, a boulder tumble, and a cow moo; but we do not necessarily listen to interpret and make sense out of these sounds. Mr. Speck has heard Harold, but he has not listened to him. He has allowed his eyes to prejudice his ears—one of the commoner errors that contribute to inefficient listening.

> Mr. Speck nods as though he understands. He reads more of Harold's application, squinches up his face in thought, and begins to ask another question. But just then the softball players behind the placement office erupt into a horrendous shout as the tying run steals third. Mr. Speck adjusts his glasses and strokes his chin, and begins to frame the question again, when the pesky fly suddenly lands on his bald head and begins to clean its feet. Mr. Speck swats at the fly, bangs his own head, frowns, mops his sweaty face, and asks: "Why do you want to work for Acme Office Supply?"
>
> Harold replies, "I think it's a pretty good company. It's the third largest in the area and I think I'd have a good future working for a company of that size."
>
> Mr. Speck hears: "I don't really give a hoot who I work for, really. I just need a job."

Commentary: Physical environment often affects the listener's interpretation of a message

In this case, neither Harold's hair nor his mustache caused Mr. Speck's misinterpretation. Instead, the noisy softball game, the hot room, and the dive-bombing fly have clouded Mr. Speck's senses to the point that he is scarcely listening to Harold. Most of us, no doubt, have been in a situation where unpleasant surroundings have prevented us from listening attentively. Crammed into a crowded church pew during 100°F weather, even a saint would have trouble listening to a sermon. If intelligent listening is to take place, the listeners must be comfortable. If they aren't, they will squirm, fidget, and daydream about escape, rather than listen.

Listening, moreover, takes place at a very slow pace. Speakers ordinarily talk between 140 to 180 words per minute; the mind can think considerably faster—up to 600 words per minute or more. The listener's mind must therefore slow from its naturally faster pace, which is like asking a rabbit to walk like a snail. Add to this unnatural slowing down the many distractions that can come from unpleasant surroundings, and before long the mind is spinning daydreams about seashores and mountain meadows, and ignoring the speaker altogether.

> Mr. Speck has made up his mind not to give Harold the job, but his conscience will trouble him if he doesn't go through the motions of giving a fair interview. He ponders Harold's application, as though he's giving it deep thought. In fact, as he reads he's saying to himself, "This guy joked around for five years and now he gets out of school and thinks he's going to grab the first job that comes along. After spending five years trying to tear down the country, he now wants to leech off of it." Then, Mr. Speck asks Harold: "Were you a member of any fraternities while you were in school?"
>
> Harold replies: "No. I was too busy trying to earn enough to pay rent and buy food. I didn't have time to join anything."
>
> A lifetime member of the Sigma Apple Pie, Mr. Speck answers mentally for Harold this way: "Naw, I didn't join any fraternities. I was too busy demonstrating against everything rotten in American society to join anything as respectable and decent as a fraternity."

Commentary: Listeners who mentally argue against a speaker during a speech often hear only themselves

There is nothing profound nor mysterious about this observation, yet arguing against a speaker before the speaker is done is often a major obstacle to efficient listening. Everyone deserves a day in court—the speaker on the platform no less than the neighbor complaining about your noisy dog. In each case, your obligation is to listen. There is plenty of time to rebut later, when he or she is finished talking. By listening to the entire speech, you get the whole story, not a fragment.

Ten minutes later, the interview was done. Mr. Speck and Harold shook hands and went their respective ways. Harold went home to tell his landlady that he thought he'd be able to pay her something next month for he was sure he'd just landed a job. Mr. Speck went to his office and wrote a report that he'd just interviewed a closet radical who wouldn't last at Acme. Ten days later, Harold received a form letter from Acme, regretting that the position had been filled.

The above story is true. Harold got a job with another company in the office supply business and, two years later as a successful salesman for a competitor to Acme, met Mr. Speck over a cup of coffee. Mr. Speck explained why he had not hired Harold, much to the latter's astonishment. When Mr. Speck was done explaining, Harold stared at him with amazement and exclaimed: "But I never said anything like that!"

HOW TO BECOME A MORE EFFICIENT LISTENER

The good news is that listening behavior can be dramatically improved if you are willing to work at it. But improvement will not come easily. You will have to get into the habit of doing a very difficult thing: being fair. Efficient listening involves the temporary suspension of prejudice, snap judgments, and personal preferences. Judgment and preferences are not chucked out for good, merely set aside so that you can listen wholeheartedly to the speaker. You must blot out noise and distraction, force your mind to keep pace with the rate at which the speaker is talking, and squash all daydreaming about seashores and mountain meadows. And, most difficult of all, you must mentally adjust to the speaker's baggy pants, which you may despise, to his nervous tic, which makes you cringe, and to all the other human afflictions that may affect his delivery. All these prescriptions basically boil down to being fair. We will list them systematically, though the entire catalog should occur to any fair-minded person.

Prepare yourself to listen

Focus your mind on the process of listening. Convince yourself beforehand of the necessity of hearing out the speaker. Mentally blot out any noise, movement, or other distraction that may interfere with your listening. Try to find a seat or place that suits you. Make whatever comfort adjustments you have to before the speaker begins.

Don't mentally argue with the speaker

When we hear a speaker arguing for an idea that contradicts our values, our first impulse is to counterattack. But if you're fair, you'll give speakers a chance to present their views before you set out to refute them. There are at least two good reasons why you should allow speakers to have their say: It gives you a chance to assess the entire case, to weigh all the evidence, and to examine all the arguments; it gives you an opportunity to be logically persuaded.

All of us change our minds at one time or another. The brain is soft and squishy like an amoeba, not rock-hard and stiff like a bone. Sooner or later, the brain will find a new notion pleasing, and establish it among its catalog of values. But if we systematically blot out anything we hear that we find disagreeable, we deny ourselves the opportunity to change and run the risk of becoming boneheads.

Compensate for the speaker's delivery

Some brilliant men and women have been poor speakers. Einstein was never as persuasive as a good used-car dealer. Oliver Goldsmith, the English writer and poet, was notoriously tongue-tied. Nevertheless, Einstein propounded his famous theory of relativity, and Goldsmith composed his witty comedy *She Stoops to Conquer*. The point is that many speakers who make a good deal of sense may express themselves badly. Scarcely anything is quite as annoying as the speaker who mumbles, stares at his feet, hems and haws, scratches his nose, or does any number of other annoying things while speaking. Nonetheless, you must remind yourself that you have come to listen to the speaker's words, not to admire his elocutionary genius. Have compassion; be patient. You must compensate for the defects in delivery, or, at least, not allow these defects to color your interpretation of the speech.

Don't undermine the speaker's message

If you cling vehemently to some ideology, you are probably already a fanatic and might as well skip this section. Some ideologies assume that only the enlightened know their own minds, and that everyone else is either duped or self-deluded. For instance, a fundamentalist Christian, hearing a talk on evolution, might dismiss the speaker as possessed of the devil; a Marxist might damn a speaker as a capitalistic dupe; a Freudian might take everything a speaker says as a sign of a mother-complex. The mind in the grip of any rigid ideology hears only itself talking. Again, we are back to the fundamental principle of being fair, of assessing an argument by its evidence and logic.

Don't lose your temper over words

There are *god* words and *devil* words. *Devil* words, for us, sum up a great wickedness in the world; *god* words represent a great good. To a prude, *pornography* might be a devil word; to the pornographer, the devil word might be *censorship*. *Motherhood* used to be a god word, although nowadays some circles regard it as a devil word. *Patriotism, free enterprise, freedom* are commonly regarded as god words; *communism, welfare state, socialism* are frequently used devil words. It depends, of course, on what you believe.

In any event, the danger is that these words will either goad you into a temper, or lull you into a state of bliss, with the same result in each case—critical thinking is abandoned. You either rage mentally at the speaker or you itch to burst into applause. The aim of efficient listening is neither to wildly praise nor to fiercely damn any speaker, but to critically examine concepts, arguments, and evidence with logic and reason.

Take notes

Note-taking is one way of occupying a mind that is threatening to outrace a speaker. In addition, it leaves you with a record that you can critically review after the speaker is finished. There are numerous forms of note-taking, and many students devise systems of their own. The synopsis method, which assembles major ideas and concepts in an outline, is probably the easiest and most useful. Here is an example. If the original speech reads like this:

> We do not know as much about these aborigines of Jamaica as we would like. They had no form of writing and so left no written record. A certain amount of information is contained in the books about the era by early Spanish visitors, beginning with Columbus himself, who, in his account of his first voyage of discovery, gives a vivid description of his meeting with the Arawak Indians and of all that was new and striking to European eyes. A

good deal of evidence was left by the Indians, of course, in the form of refuse heaps, or "middens" as they are called, in pottery remains, stone implements, wood, stone and rock carvings, idols and ornaments, even in their own skeletons. From careful study of these remains much information has come to light and archaeologists are constantly adding to our knowledge.[5]

The outline would synopsize it something like this:

> Jamaican aborigines—little known
>   No written Indian record
>   Information from Spanish writing, Columbus on Arawaks
> Indian evidence
>   Refuse heaps—*middens*
>   Pottery, stone artifacts, skeletons
>   Archaeologists use these

One-hundred-fourteen words are condensed to a twenty-eight word synopsis. This sort of outline, used with an ordinary recollection of a speaker's words, can usually give a fairly accurate record of a speech.

Note-taking, like many other skills, improves with practice. The principle, however, is simply to list the speaker's ideas in an outline form.

WHAT TO LISTEN FOR

Skilled listening involves more than simply leaning back in one's chair and peering owlishly at a speaker. One must listen intently, not just for every puff of breath that comes out of a speaker's mouth, but for some rather specific things in a speech. What should an alert listener listen for in a speech?

Listen for a central idea

The central idea of a speech is a statement of what the speaker intends to argue, prove, refute, or discuss. Conventionally, it is stated rather early in the speech, giving both speaker and listeners some general notion of what's to come. Without a central idea, a speech will simply leapfrog from topic to topic. Here is an example of a central idea clearly stated in a speech:

> Let me tell you the route I intend to follow in this speech which I probably should have entitled, "The First Amendment, Public Decision Making, and Television." . . . First, I intend to sketch a little theoretical background involving the implications of the First Amendment to the Constitution. Second, I intend to do a flashback and discuss how the political speaker faced the voters in pre-television days. Third, I shall consider how and why television has altered the role of the speaker and the politician.[6]

One has no doubt, from the very outset, what the speaker intends to do.

Folk wisdom tells us that some people can see individual trees, but cannot see an entire forest. The listener who, after listening to a speech, recalls its details and particular assertions but forgets its central idea, is to be numbered in this category. Such a listener has seen the trees, but missed the forest.

Listen for evidence

Impassioned speakers can easily rattle off innumerable glib assertions. "Communism is taking over the country"; "fluoride is poisoning our children"; "UFO's have invaded Connecticut"; "free love is destroying marriage." The possibilities for wild generalizations are endless. Nor, for that matter, are specious claims, vague generalizations, and empty platitudes restricted to soap box orators in parks. Eminent speakers often make equally silly and preposterous claims. The conscientious listener who does not wish to be duped by every shrieking orator must therefore listen intently for supporting evidence. If none is given, then the speaker's claim must not be believed, no matter how passionately shrieked.

But how does a listener evaluate the validity of evidence? Common sense recommends two simple tests: First, the evidence must be *appropriate* to the claim; second, the evidence must be *confirmable*. If a speaker, for instance, claims that Russia has passed the United States in military might, this contention must be supported by appropriate statistics, which measure relative military strength. Moreover, either the source of the evidence must be identified, or the evidence must be of the kind whose accuracy any interested listener can easily confirm.

The following paragraph presents evidence that is both appropriate and confirmable:

> First, TV is so expensive that it is beyond the reach of many who might seek office or contribute to our political life. In 1970, during an off-presidential election, candidates spent $158 million on political broadcasts. In that campaign the three candidates for the governorship of New York spent more than $2 million on television and radio broadcasts. Nelson Rockefeller reportedly used $6 million and utilized a staff of 370 full-time employees. A one half-minute spot announcement on the leading Baton Rouge TV station costs as much as $150 to $300 at prime time and $50 for poorest time (probably at 1:30 in the morning). To present a fifteen-minute speech on the leading channel in Baton Rouge at 7:30 p.m. cost as much as $300 to $500. To broadcast a half-hour speech over Louisiana TV networks might cost $25,000 to $30,000.[7]

The evidence, presented to support the speaker's claim that TV is too expensive for many politicians, is entirely appropriate. Although no source is cited for these figures, the evidence is confirmable. Scant research by any interested listener could easily prove or disprove the accuracy of these figures.

Dubious, unconfirmable evidence is often introduced with the innocent phrase, "it is estimated." Consider, for instance, the following assertions:

> It is estimated that by the year 1986, the Russians will possess ten times more offensive missiles than the United States, eight times more submarines, fifty times the number of conventional troops, and nearly one hundred more aircraft carriers.

In the face of such specific but unconfirmable mush, a listener's best defense is to immediately ask, "says who?" If the speech gives no definite answer, then neither the claim nor the evidence should be believed.

Not all evidence, however, is numerical. Sometimes, speakers will support their arguments by quoting the opinion of an authority. The validity of testimonial evidence—as evidence of this kind is called—depends on the credentials of the authority, and the authority's qualifications to comment as an expert on the speaker's subject. Typically, a speaker will sketch the credentials of an authority before quoting the authority's opinion. Here are two examples:

> John Goodland, dean of the UCLA College of Education, concluded that schools are "anything but the palaces of an affluent society."

> What I am saying was recently confirmed by a published interview with Alistair Cooke, chief U.S. Correspondent for *The Guardian,* one of England's most distinguished newspapers . . . (followed by Cooke's opinion of American television)

In these two cases, a dean of a college of education is presumed to be an expert on schools, and a journalist to be an expert on television.

Testimonial evidence is often misused by speakers eager to shout out the opinion of any well-known person sympathetic to their cause. But an authority in one field, no matter with what sterling credentials, is not necessarily an authority in another. Goodland, an authority on education, is no authority on television; Cooke, an authority on television, is no authority on education. Likewise, Ralph Nader may be an authority on consumer issues, but he is no authority on nuclear engineering. John Wayne may be renowned for gunning down fictional bad guys, but his background hardly qualifies him as an authority on pain-relievers. Confronted with testimonial evidence, wary listeners should not only listen for the credentials of the authority, but should also inquire whether the authority is, in fact, qualified as an expert on the speaker's subject.

Listen for definitions

A definition is a statement of what a thing is, or of what a word or expression means. Many of us naively assume that all people subscribe to the dictionary meanings of words. Not only is this often not the case, but it is frequently impossible for antagonistic factions to agree even on the meanings of ordinary words. For instance, during the 1960s, the seemingly innocuous and straightforward phrase "law and order" became such a polarizing expression that Richard

Nixon, in his presidential nomination acceptance speech delivered at Miami Beach on August 8th, 1968, was obliged to say:

> And to those who say that law and order is the code word for racism, here is a reply: Our goal is justice—justice for every American. If we are to have respect for law in America, we must have laws that deserve respect. Just as we cannot have progress without order, we cannot have order without progress.

Semanticists divide words into two general groups: concrete words and abstract words. Concrete words stand for physical entities. A speaker says that yesterday he was bitten by a dachshund. If his listeners quibble about the meaning of "dachshund," the argument can be settled by showing the dog. Abstract words, on the other hand, indicate the invisible, the unseen, the imaginary, and the purely conceptual. "Freedom" has no corporeal form that can be shown; "love" has smitten many, but none have ever seen it. Speakers who use abstract terms are therefore obliged to define them—especially when such terms are crucial to the subject of the speech. Listeners, for their part, who mishear these definitions, could completely misunderstand the meaning of the speech.

Here is an example that illustrates the importance of definitions in a speech. A speaker declares that "manners are a sign of education," and then goes on to say what he means by *manners:*

> "Manners are behavior and good breeding," as Addison said, but they are more. It is not without significance that the Latin language has but a single word (mores) both for usages, habits, manners, and for morals. Real manners, the manners of a truly educated man or woman, are an outward expression of intellectual and moral conviction. Sham manners are a veneer which falls away at the dampening touch of the first selfish suggestion. Manners have a moral significance, and find their basis in that true and deepest self-respect which is built upon respect for others. An infallible test of character is to be found in one's manners towards those whom, for one reason or another, the world may deem his inferiors. A man's manners towards his equals or his superiors are shaped by too many motives to render their interpretation either easy or certain. Manners do not make the man, but manners reveal the man.[8]

The definition goes on in considerable detail, but enough of it has been quoted here to illustrate its importance in the speech. *Manners,* as the speaker intends the word, has neither the ordinary nor dictionary meaning. The listener who missed this definition could easily misunderstand an important part of the speech.

Listen for irrelevancies

In the chapter on logic, we catalog a number of irrelevancies that speakers are fond of using. These range from irritating rambling and failure to focus on a topic, to deliberate and unfavorable characterizations of issues and persons. Basically, an irrelevancy occurs whenever a speaker departs from reasonable and logical argument. Departures can take a number of courses: Emotional side issues can be introduced and wildly trumpeted; silly generalizations can be solemnly made as though they were sacred truths. Numerous examples of these kinds of irrelevancies can be found in the speeches of eminent people who should not only know better, but do better. Here, for instance, is a vice president of the United States unfavorably characterizing the opponents of his administration's Vietnam policy:

> The student now goes to college to proclaim rather than to learn. The lessons of the past are ignored and obliterated in a contemporary antagonism known as the generation gap. A spirit of national masochism prevails, encouraged by an effete corps of impudent snobs who characterize themselves as intellectuals.[9]

Colorful language, but entirely beside the point. Such irrelevancies merely inflame, rather than inform. Intelligent listeners should never allow themselves to be beguiled by this sort of emotional claptrap.

For more information on irrelevancies in speeches, see Chapter 13.

Listen for recommendations, suggestions, and conclusions

Speakers generally give speeches with a distinct purpose in mind. The preacher wants us to walk the straight and narrow path; the politician wants our vote; the salesperson craves our order. Sometime, therefore, at the end of the speech, after the speaker has gone over what is wrong, what is deficient, what is missing, what is needed, a recommendation will more than likely be made, a solution proposed, an action suggested, or a conclusion drawn. The listener who misses this stage of a speech has dined on hors d'oeuvres but missed the entree. Here, at the conclusion of a speech on the inadequacy of inner-city schools, a speaker offers her solutions:

> A first step would be to issue federal and state appropriations to rebuild and improve schools, to furnish modern technical equipment and free meals. But no physical change will yield results unless there is a concern for the second step. Relevant teacher-training programs, classroom textbooks and materials must be redesigned with an awareness of inner-city culture. I am not suggesting that we perpetuate the cultural inadequacies of the inner-city school, but it is impossible to achieve meaningful, productive behavior in an affluent society unless you relate to and move forward from the students' own frame of reference.[10]

In many speeches, it is evident long before the end what the speaker intends to propose, recommend, or urge. Listeners must nevertheless remain alert or they may miss any unexpected or imaginative solutions that a speaker may have—the very heart and soul of a speech. Moreover, since this is the stage during which a speaker will exhort an audience to action, a listener should be especially critical and wary. You should never leap out of your chair after hearing a rousing oration and rush pell-mell into the fray. Better, instead, to slowly assimilate, weigh, and ponder the speech; to ask yourself whether the conclusions are logically drawn from the evidence; whether the proposed solutions are workable and likely to do any good; and whether the speaker's recommendations provide a reasonable, temperate answer to the problem.

NOTES

[1] Ralph G. Nichols and Leonard A. Stevens, *Are You Listening?* (New York: McGraw-Hill, 1957).

[2] According to a survey taken by the Book Manufacturers Institute. Quoted in William Norwood Brigance, *Speech: Its Techniques And*

Disciplines in a Free Society (New York: Appleton-Century-Crofts, 1961).

[3] Nichols and Stevens.

[4] Gauleiter Albert Krebs quoted in John Toland, *Adolf Hitler,* Vol. 1 (New York: Doubleday, 1976).

[5] Clinton V. Black, *The Story of Jamaica* (Cleveland, Ohio: Collins, 1973).

[6] Waldo W. Braden, "Has TV Made the Public Speaker Obsolete?" Annual Conference of the American Council for Better Broadcast, Baton Rouge, Louisiana, 25 April 1974.

[7] Braden, "Has TV Made the Public Speaker Obsolete?"

[8] Nicholas Murray Butler, "Five Evidences of an Education," address before the Phi Beta Kappa Society of Vassar College, Poughkeepsie, New York, 10 June 1901.

[9] Spiro Agnew, speaking at Citizens' Testimonial Dinner, New Orleans, Louisiana, 19 October 1969.

[10] Patricia Warren, "Bring Forth the Children, Interstate Oratorical Association contest, 1971.

BIBLIOGRAPHY

Barbara, Dominick A., *The Act of Listening* (Springfield, Illinois: Charles C. Thomas, Inc., 1958).

Barker, Larry L., *Listening Behavior* (Englewood Cliffs, N.J.: Prentice-Hall, 1971).

Johnson, Wendell, *Your Most Enchanted Listener* (New York: Harper & Row, 1956).

Kelley, Charles M., "Emphatic Listening," in *Concepts in Communication,* ed. Jimmie D. Trent et al. (Boston: Allyn & Bacon, 1973).

Nichols, Ralph G. and Leonard A. Stevens, *Are You Listening?* (New York: McGraw-Hill, 1957).

Weaver, Carl, *Human Listening: Processes and Behavior* (Indianapolis: Bobbs-Merrill, 1972).

Coping with speechfright

Confidence is inspired by the remoteness of calamities and by the proximity of sources of encouragement.

—Aristotle

DEFINITION OF SPEECHFRIGHT

Speechfright refers to the fear or timidity a speaker experiences before an audience, and a majority of us—if we have ever had to speak in public—have at one time or another suffered from it.

We are not alone. The same flutters have attacked a nearly endless list of luminaries. Abraham Lincoln used to grimace and shake the first few minutes of his every address.[1] Sir Laurence Olivier, tormented by preperformance jitters, would often pace backstage and curse his audience. Called out of the audience and asked to make a speech while attending the theater, Washington Irving rushed from the building and immediately fled town.[2] William Jennings Bryan, Mark Twain, Jack Benny, Jane Fonda, and Ulysses S. Grant all suffered speechfright of varying severity. And, attesting to how widespread an affliction speechfright is, the *Sunday Times,* London (7 October 1973), lists the following fourteen worst human fears, compiled from a survey of 3000 U.S. inhabitants:

Biggest fear	Percent naming
1. Speaking before a group	41
2. Heights	32
3. Insects and bugs	22
3. Financial problems	22
3. Deep water	22
6. Sickness	19
6. Death	19
8. Flying	18
9. Loneliness	14
10. Dogs	11
11. Driving/riding in a car	9
12. Darkness	8
12. Elevators	8
14. Escalators	5

Although astonishing, it is evidently true: Many Americans fear speaking in public more than financial ruin, sickness, or death. Other surveys have confirmed that students are similarly afraid of speaking before an audience. Of the students questioned in one survey, 60 percent to 75 percent admitted to nervousness; of these, 35 percent regarded their nervousness as severe.[3]

SYMPTOMS OF SPEECHFRIGHT

Speechfright, as the second half of the word indicates, is a fear response. Perceiving a threatening situation, the brain mobilizes the body for flight, aggression or attack. Biochemical reactions—the same that helped early humans outrun rogue dinosaurs and battle rampaging sabre-tooth tigers—are set into effect. Adrenalin and thyroxin are dumped into the bloodstream, causing the heartbeat to race and the blood pressure to rise. The pupils of the eyes dilate; the liver pumps sugar into the blood, increasing available energy. Diverted from the stomach and the intestines, blood is shuttled to the brain and skeletal muscles, and its clotting ability increases. Digestion churns to a halt. Respiration speeds up; hairs stand on end, causing a rash of "goosepimples." The glandular, vascular, and muscular systems go on a "red alert" status.

The stricken speaker, whose brain has involuntarily readied his body for physical combat, is merely standing on stage quivering at a sea of peering faces. Yet he has the distinct impression that his body has gone mad and is certain that even as he stands at the podium, the audience can hear his heart thumping and can see every bone in his body trembling. In sum, the speaker's consciousness of his own frantic physiological responses further adds to his fear, beginning a vicious cycle.

The visible signs of severe speechfright are numerous but classifiable. Any of the following symptoms may occur, either separately or in combination:

Voice:	1.	Quivers
	2.	Too fast
	3.	Too slow
	4.	Monotonous; unemphatic
Verbal fluency:	5.	Stammers; halting
	6.	Awkward pauses
	7.	Hunts for words; speech blocked
Mouth and throat:	8.	Swallows repeatedly
	9.	Clears throat repeatedly
	10.	Breathes heavily
Facial expression:	11.	No eye contact; rolls eyes
	12.	Tense face muscles; grimaces; twitches
	13.	Deadpan expression
Arms and hands:	14.	Rigid or tense
	15.	Fidgets; waves hands about
	16.	Motionless; stiff
Gross body movements:	17.	Sways; paces; shuffles feet[4]

But how does it all appear, audience, auditorium, moderator, to a speaker stricken with severe speechfright? A vivid description was written in the nineteenth century by Angelo Mosso, a professor of physiology, who was appearing in public to lecture on the physiology of sleep:

> Never shall I forget that evening! From behind the curtains of a glass door I peered into the large amphitheater crowded with people. It was my first appearance as a lecturer, and most humbly did I repent having undertaken to try my powers in the same

hall in which my most celebrated teachers had so often spoken. All I had to do was to communicate the results of some of my investigations into the physiology of sleep, and yet, as the hour drew nearer, stronger waxed within me the fear that I should become confused, lose myself, and finally stand gaping, speechless before my audience. My heart beat violently, its very strings seemed to tighten, and my breath came and went, as when one looks down into a yawning abyss. At last it struck eight. As I cast a last glance at my notes, I became aware, to my horror, that the chain of ideas was broken and the links lost beyond recall. Experiments performed a hundred times, long periods which I had thought myself able to repeat word for word—all seemed forgotten, swept away as though it had never been.

Eventually, the terrified Mosso mounted the platform and began his talk.

How strange was the sound of my first words! My voice seemed to lose itself in a great wilderness; words, scarce fallen from my lips, to tremble and die away. After a few sentences jerked out almost mechanically, I perceived that I had already finished the introduction to my speech, and discovered with dismay that memory had played me false just at the point where I had thought myself most sure; but there was no turning back, and so, in great confusion, I proceeded. The hall seemed enveloped in mist. Slowly the cloud began to lift, and here and there in the crowd I could distinguish benevolent, friendly faces, and on these I fixed my gaze, as a man struggling with waves clings to a floating spar. I could discern, too, the attentive countenances of eager listeners, holding a hand to their ear as though unwilling to lose a single word, and nodding occasionally in token of affirmation. And lastly, I saw myself in this semicircle, alone, humbled, discouraged, dejected—like a sinner at confession.

Mosso stumbled through his lecture, beleagured throughout by severe speechfright, noting at the end:

I was perspiring, exhausted, my strength was failing; I glanced at the tier of seats, and it seemed to me that they were slowly opening in front of me, like the jaws of a monster ready to devour me as soon as the last word should re-echo within its throat.[5]

Inspired partly by the memory of that dreadful evening, Mosso went on to do some pioneering research on the psychology of fear, about which he eventually wrote a book.

CAUSES OF SPEECHFRIGHT

There are several theories, depending on which school of psychology one consults, about what causes speechfright. An early study linked speechfright to a trauma previously suffered by a speaker while giving a speech.[6] A woman, for instance, was said to have contracted severe speechfright because she discovered that her slip was showing while she addressed a group. Never again was she able to give a speech without reliving the trauma and embarrassment of that original incident. But the trauma theory, while no doubt applicable to some severe cases, cannot account for the innumerable reported cases of speechfright experienced by even hardened public speakers. It is simply too farfetched to believe that so many people have suffered early public speaking traumas.

Emotion

Some writers account for speechfright with an explanation that has its roots in the controversial James/Lange theory of emotion—named for the psychologists who advanced it, William James and Carl Lange. Basically, this theory says that emotion results not from physiological activity, but from *an awareness of emotion.* To illustrate this subtle distinction, James cites the instance of a man walking in the woods who suddenly encounters a bear. Perceiving the bear as a danger, the man's brain immediately prepares the body for an emergency by putting the muscular, glandular, and vascular systems on the "red alert status" described earlier. The heartbeat and pulse races; the bloodstream is flooded with adrenalin and thyroxin; in short, the man meeting the bear feels very much like a speaker mounting a dais to give a speech. According to the James/Lange theory, this instantaneous readiness of the body to cope with the bear is a normal and useful reaction that cannot be regarded as emotion anymore than a cramp in one's tummy. What frightens the man is not so much the bear as his awareness of his body's sudden and urgent reactions to it. The man's perception that his body has gone into a state of controlled frenzy is therefore the *real emotion.*

This explanation, controversial or not, is unquestionably applicable to a nervous speaker giving a speech. Half the battle against speechfright would be won if a speaker could regard his nervous qualms with the same composure as he views a stomach cramp. But this is seldom the case. What often upsets a speaker most is the uncomfortable awareness of a feeling of utter panic. That awareness is the *real emotion*. A speaker finds it especially unnerving to hear the frantic thumping of his heart, and imagines that his dreadful fear is plainly visible to the audience.

Often, however, a speaker's fear, though sincerely felt, is not visible. Even experienced speech teachers cannot always tell that a speaker is suffering from speechfright.[7] One study found that the more skillful the presentation of a speaker, the less likely an audience would perceive the speaker's nervousness.[8] The implication is that though your heart may be thumping mightily as you give the speech, if you have done your homework and rehearsed the speech diligently, the audience is not likely to notice any speechfright symptoms.

An increasingly popular view of speechfright argues that a modicum of nervousness is perfectly normal in any speaker. One researcher put it this way: "To experience nervousness while giving a public speech is normal."[9] Another was more elaborate:

> "Speech anxiety" is not a pathological phenomenon derived from some personality quirk. The student knows, for example, why he is apprehensive; he is fearful, not anxious in an irrational, personality-trait, or pathological sense.[10]

But this sort of explanation is roundabout. To say that speechfright is normal is merely to say that most speakers suffer from it. Something similar can be said about colds in winter—that they are frequent and widespread and many people get them. Nevertheless, there must be a reason for speechfright. One suggestion might be that the experience of giving a public speech is frightening because it activates unwritten fears in our culture against strangers, staring, and novelty.

Fear of strangers

Most of us grew up being warned by our parents not to speak to strangers. It is a rule we observe from childhood into adulthood and even pass on to our own children. We chat amiably with a friend in a line at the supermarket, but stand aloof and speechless if the line is filled with strangers. It has been recently suggested that this fear of strangers may be learned in early infancy. Laboratory studies reveal that infants up to four months old will readily smile at strangers; inexplicably, this behavior changes dramatically when the infant is six months old.[11] A similar receptivity to strange faces and objects also occurs in very young animals and just as abruptly changes as they grow older.[12] Public speaking, which often involves addressing a group of strangers, no doubt evokes this ancient fear, adding significantly to the speaker's nervousness.

Fear of staring

Staring is universally feared by both humans and animals. Often, the stare is used to signal a threat. Many animals scare off intruders into their territory by staring.[13] In her study of baboons, Jane Goodall found that ambitious male baboons would start a fight for herd dominance by staring at the leader. If the leader returned the stare, the challenge was accepted, and the fight would immediately begin. Goodall also found that any aging, shaky leader who was unsure of his fighting abilities would go to great pretences to avoid meeting a stare, even if the challenger's face was thrust only inches away from his nose, as it often would be. The leader would yawn, close his eyes, stare up at the sky, or pretend to be fascinated with some object on the ground.[14] If we are to believe cowboy movies, the gunslinger, like the baboon, also issued challenges with a stare. "What are you looking at?" one gunfighter would demand of another who was raking him with a beady gaze. From this to "Draw," or some such earthy invitation, is only a mouthful of popcorn away.

Giving a speech involves getting up before a crowd of strangers and being unrelentingly stared at. The speaker, unlike an aging baboon leader, cannot, without seeming silly, go through gyrations to avoid meeting the stares of the audience. Standing on the platform before dozens, even hundreds, of staring eyes, the speaker must casually ignore their stares and go on with the speech. No one can say exactly to what extent this staring contributes to a speaker's feelings of nervousness. But, given the universal fear of staring, a good guess would be that the effect is considerable.

Fear of novelty

Finally, there is the fear of the novel, a fear that most of us have experienced at one time or another. Psychologists and writers have recorded instances of it in fact and fiction. It is a real fear in the animal kingdom and has been observed in ravens, chimpanzees, and rhesus monkeys.[15] Animals exposed to objects they have never seen before generally react with panic and threats. Children evidence fear of the novel and react to it with varying degrees of curiosity and terror. Most of us can remember vividly the fear and exhilaration we felt over "first time" experiences—the first time we rode a bicycle, drove a car, went out on a date, or traveled alone. With repetition these experiences and events soon become as familiar, humdrum, and commonplace as anything else we've been doing for years.

Whatever else a speech may be, it is assuredly a novel event. Most of us have given few speeches; some of us have never given a speech. When we are asked to give a speech, there is enough of the novel in the occasion to cause our hearts to thump and our palms to sweat. We must address strangers; be remorselessly stared at; expose ourselves to a novel situation whose outcome is uncertain. Granted, we might be a colossal hit; on the other hand, we might be an ignominious flop. The situation is fraught with uncertainty and peril. We begin to wonder how we will react, whether we will make a fool of ourselves. Before we know what's happening, we are dreading the approach of the speech. Our hearts palpitate at the very thought of giving it; by the time we mount the podium, we are experiencing the symptoms of speechfright.

HOW TO COPE WITH SPEECHFRIGHT

Understand and accept it.

There is no magical cure for speechfright. Neither elixir, physician, nor astrologer can make it completely go away. If you have to give speeches, you will most likely suffer some symptoms of speechfright. Your heart may beat a trifle faster; your palms may perspire a little; your knees may quiver and knock a bit. But a little speechfright is not entirely a bad thing. William Cullen Bryant, in his day one of America's best-loved speakers, once said that if the time ever came when he could walk in front of an audience and not feel speechfright, he would think that he was losing the necessary equipment for giving speeches.

Use your fear energy

No doubt, Bryant had recognized a paradox of human physiology, namely, that with fear come extraordinary bursts of energy. We have all heard stories about ordinary people who have scaled ten-foot fences in one stupendous leap while being chased by a bull; about mothers who have lifted impossible weights to rescue their children; about husbands who have run into fiery buildings and emerged dragging their unconscious wives. Adrenalin and thyroxin are generally responsible for these feats. These hormones snap the physiological functions into a peak state of readiness and render the ordinary person capable of amazing acts of strength and energy. Likewise adrenalin and thyroxin give the speaker the burst of energy necessary for effective communication with an audience.

Giving an effective public speech requires far more energy and strength than holding a conversation with friends. Impassioned orators have been known to shed ten pounds after one hour at the podium. The bigger the audience, the more of themselves speakers must project. They must concentrate on what they have to say, articulate loud enough to be heard in the back row, establish eye contact with the audience, emphasize their points with appropriate gestures, and—at the same time—be sensitive to audience feedback. In sum, the speaker must be extraordinarily alert to a degree impossible without the bursts of energy provided by adrenalin and thyroxin —the same hormones responsible for the symptoms of fear.

When you have to make a speech, therefore, don't grit your teeth and fight against your nervousness. Don't scowl at your image in the mirror and berate yourself for being fearful. You'll only make yourself tenser than you already are. Accept the presence of speechfright as a positive sign that adrenalin and thyroxin are giving you the energy boost necessary to deliver a rousing speech.

Choose a topic you like

Enthusiasm over a speech topic can sometimes cause speakers to forget their nervousness. If you've chosen a topic that you're really excited about, chances are that once you begin the speech your speechfright will rapidly fade. Enthusiasm, in any event, tends to be contagious, and should help improve the quality of your speech and your contact with the audience, even if it doesn't allay your nervousness.

This rather self-evident prescription seems not to occur to many students, for few, indeed, appear to follow it. Many students grab on to the first convenient and easy topic that comes to mind, regardless of whether or not it appeals to them. Speechfright is made worse by a poor topic choice, because once the pressures and jitters of giving the speech descend on the poor students, they are further bothered by having to slog through a humdrum topic they care nothing about.

The advice to choose a topic you're enthusiastic about is well worth heeding.

Be prepared

For many students, speechfright is really a thinly disguised fear of ridicule and failure. Nothing protects against failure better than practice. Once the topic is chosen, the evidence gathered, the speech outlined, and the ideas arranged, the next three steps—especially for the fearful student—should be practice, practice, and practice. The point is not to rote memorize every word of the speech, which would probably result in a wooden and robotlike performance. Instead, practice involves thoroughly digesting the major points of the speech and the sequence in which you intend to make them. It means conducting several "dry runs" through the speech until you're certain that no matter how your heart pitter-patters, you'll still be able to deliver your speech. Here is the regimen of practice one prominent business speaker adopted for himself:

I would stand in front of the mirror and watch my delivery. I would ask everybody for ideas for improvement.

It was good training, I found quickly, to give my speech before a mirror. Here I saw myself as others were seeing me, and I learned a lot.

I saw mistakes I was making in facial gestures, in dress, in actions. I often felt disgusted with myself, for the mirror is honest and tells the truth. One day I noticed that my necktie was so loud I could hardly see my face, so I started wearing a more conservative tie. Then I decided upon a bow tie so that the white of my shirt would highlight my face even more. I practiced, for only by practice could I improve.

At times I found my breath was in my throat, as I became enthusiastic and took a deep breath. One day I was told to breathe from the diaphragm.

It took several weeks before it became a normal thing with me, but it sure kept the wind in my chest to sound off with, rather than in my throat to choke me.

As I look back at those first five years of struggling to be a success on the platform, I'd say here is a third great rule for learning the art of speaking in public: *Make daily and excellent use of your mirror.* [Author's italics.][16]

Practice will make you confident. Devise your own practice sessions and follow them religiously until you're reassured that no matter how frightened you become, you'll still be able to give the speech.

Exercise to release tension

While you are waiting in class for your turn to make a speech, you cannot, of course, flop down on the floor to do push-ups or sit-ups. However, if you are really attacked by the jitters and feel terribly tense, you can quietly do some isometric exercises that may help you to relax. Isometric exercises are done by tensing the muscles against each other or against an immovable object. For instance, you can exercise the muscles of both arms by placing your palms squarely against each other and pushing as hard as you can. An individual muscle can be quietly exercised by contracting the muscle for a few seconds and then abruptly releasing it.

Bear in mind that the point of these exercises is to help a frightened, tense student relax. Sometimes, the interminable waiting for one's turn to make a speech can be sheer torture. By quietly exercising as you sit and wait, you may ease your tension and take your mind off the long walk to the podium. A good mental exercise to keep your mind off the upcoming speech is active listening. Instead of simply sitting in your chair and worrying about how well you'll do when your turn comes, concentrate on the speeches of the other students. Ponder each point; query the supporting evidence; take notes on content; analyze the delivery of the speaker. If you concentrate on listening, you're less likely to sit and brood and make your speechfright worse.

Desensitize your speechfright

Desensitizing procedures can be used to rid a speaker of severe speechfright. The speaker is exposed gradually to tiny increments of the speechmaking process. When the speaker has become accustomed to one increment, he is exposed to another, until the speechfright is gradually lessened.

If the entire class can be involved in a desensitizing attempt, we suggest the following procedures. (If the entire class will not be involved, we suggest you arrange with a group of mutually frightened students, find an empty classroom, and follow the recommended program on your own.)

1. Students take turns reading aloud while sitting in their accustomed places. This step gets students used to talking to the entire class, but spares them the ordeal of having to stand at the lectern and be stared at. Repeat this step until students are able to read freely to the class without feeling panicked.

2. Students take turns standing silently at the lectern. This step accustoms them to standing in front of the class and being the object of attention. Repeat until each student can do it comfortably.

3. Students take turns standing before the class and reading something that was never intended to be read aloud—the side panel from a cereal box, a paragraph from a college catalog, the instructions for assembling a bicycle. This step accustoms students to standing before the class and vocalizing, but spares them the stress of having to improvise. Repeat until each student can do this in a casual and relaxed way.

4. Students take turns standing before the class and reciting any short, memorized passage, preferably a nursery rhyme or jingle. This step is similar to step 3, except that the student is now reciting from memory, which more closely approximates actual speechmaking. Repeat as often as necessary until students can perform this step comfortably.

5. Students take turns giving short, prepared summaries of a news story, the plot from a television show, or the main idea from a book. Repeat with different material of gradually increasing length until students are comfortable.

You will find that it is probably impossible to conduct a program of this sort without a good deal of mirth and banter from class members. Never mind; mirth is a good antidote for speechfright. Once the class understands the purpose of the program and begins to associate fun and excitement with speechmaking, the students will be well on their way to overcoming speechfright.

NOTES

[1] Mildred F. Berry, *History and Criticism of American Public Address* (New York: McGraw-Hill, 1943), p. 847.

[2] Van Wyck Brooks, *The World of Washington Irving* (New York: E. P. Dutton, 1944), p. 36.

[3] R. S. Ross, "Survey of Incidence of Stagefright," unpublished research, Wayne State University, 1961.

[4] Adapted from A. Mulac and A. R. Sherman, "Behavioral Assessment of Speech Anxiety," *Quarterly Journal of Speech,* 60 (April 1974), pp. 134–43.

[5] Angelo Mosso, *Fear* (New York: Longmans, Green & Co., 1896), pp. 1–4.

[6] M. L. Goodhue, *The Cure of Stagefright* (Boston: The Four Seas Company, 1927), Ch. 2.

[7] E. C. Buehler, "Progress Report of Survey of Individual Attitudes and Concepts Concerning Elements Which Make for Effective Speaking," report, University of Kansas, 1958.

[8] Anthony A. Mulac and Robert Sherman, "Relationships Among Four Parameters of Speaker Evaluation: Speech Skill, Source Credibility, Subjective Speech Anxiety, and Behavioral Speech Anxiety," *Speech Monographs,* 42 (November 1975), pp. 302–10.

[9] James C. McCroskey, "Classroom Consequences of Communication Anxiety," *Communication Education,* 26 (January 1977), p. 27.

[10] D. Thomas Porter, "Self-Report Scales of Communication Apprehension and Autonomic Arousal: A Test of Construct Validity," paper presented at the Speech Communication Association Convention, New York, November 1973.

[11] Isaac M. Marks, *Fears and Phobias* (New York: Academic Press, 1969), p. 25.

[12] Marks, p. 24.

[13] Marks, p. 30.

[14] Jane Goodall, "Baboon Behavior," lecture given at Beckman Auditorium, California Institute of Technology, Pasadena, 11 December 1974.

[15] Marks, p. 27.

[16] Elmer Wheeler, *How I Mastered My Fear of Public Speaking,* (New York: Harper & Row, 1957).

2

SPEECH PREPARATION AND DELIVERY

CHAPTER

The topic and the central idea

Before beginning, prepare carefully.
—Cicero

PRACTICAL PREPARATION

There are many stories told about the reactions of famous people when unexpectedly called on to give speeches. As mentioned in
Chapter 3, the bashful Washington Irving was supposed to have instantly fled theatre, town, and state. Called upon to make a speech at
a banquet given in his honor by a scientific society, Einstein got up
and said quite simply, "I have nothing to say. When I do, I will
come back and say it." Several months later, he did.

Students faced with having to prepare their first speech for a
public speaking class will probably turn green with envy over the
ease with which Einstein got out of it. Doubtless, the great, the celebrated, the famous, can flee or simply say "no." But the student,
crammed between rows seven and eight of the classroom, cannot use
some grand gesture to avoid making a speech. When given an assignment for a speech, the student has to do it, and that's that.

But there is a sensible and nearly painless way to go about
preparing a speech, which this and the chapters that follow will systematically teach.

The speech grade

Although teachers generally know what they want from student speeches, no universal criteria for grading speeches exist. Ordinarily criteria for grading evaluate the structure of a speech, its language, its development, its presentation, and the support mustered behind its various points. But just in case your teacher might be giving more weight to one of these categories over another, ask for the grading criteria. The teacher will most likely eagerly explain them in the hope of getting a better speech.

Choosing a topic

A speech assignment may be given with or without a tailor-made topic. If the assignment comes with a specific topic, then you simply can begin gathering information about it. However, considerable freedom is generally allowed students in the selection of topics. Consequently the following section of this chapter provides guidelines for choosing speech topics. Some obvious do's and don't's on topic selection should be observed. First, the don't's.

Topics to avoid

Under this general heading fall various horrible topic choices, which students should do their utmost to avoid.

Topics that are too technical   If you choose a technical topic for your speech, you are electing to cross the ocean in a leaky boat. You might make it across, but the odds are good that you'll sink before you're halfway there. First of all, technical topics bore the typical layman. Second, technical topics usually require a technical vocabulary, which means that the speech will be riddled with asides defining and explaining the technical terms. Third, technical topics often cannot be adequately explained without charts, graphs, statistics, and illustrations, all of which conspire to do in an audience. Stay away from a technical topic even if it happens to be your pet subject. The following are examples of excessively technical topics:

> The impact of Heisenberg's principle of indeterminacy on subparticle research
>
> Fifty variations on the Sicilian defense in chess

Archetypal criticism of twentieth-century literature

The spinal cord of Hadrosaurus

A topic that in itself is not excessively technical, may be too technically treated. Most people, for instance, are aware of astrology and may even read their horoscopes in the daily newspapers. But if you gave a talk on "The meaning of astrological aspects," and spoke about the trines, squares, conjunctions, oppositions, and sextiles in considerable detail, you would probably be telling your listeners much more than they ever wanted to know about astrology.

Topics that are too broad   The important newsworthy issues are constantly on our minds nowadays, possibly because they are the subject of daily chit-chat on television and radio. Most of us have a smattering of knowledge about the nuclear testing issue, the Panama Canal question, and the feminist movement. Consequently these are the first topics to pop into our minds when we have to give a speech. But let's face it, five to seven minutes—the time allowed for the typical in-class speech—is simply not enough time to accommodate a speech on one of these large issues. Moreover, big issues are impossible to research, and difficult to digest. Use your common sense in deciding if a topic is too big. No exact rule of thumb exists, but here are some examples of topics that are simply too big to be sensibly covered in a classroom speech:

Discrimination against homosexuals throughout history

Black civil rights movements from Revolutionary days to the 1970s

Feminism in global perspective

Why wars are fought

It is far better to choose a narrower topic that can be adequately covered within the allotted speaking time than to try and subdue a gargantuan topic within the fleeting span of five minutes.

Trivial topics   Triviality, like beauty, lies in the eye of the beholder. Consequently some commonsense reflection may be required to avoid the mistake of selecting a topic important to you, but trivial to your audience. For instance, if 99 percent of an audience are men, it is highly likely that they will regard a speech topic on "How Hemlines Change" as trivial. Likewise, an audience made up preponderantly of dyed-in-the-wool Republicans is unlikely to regard as important a speech on the topic of "Affirmative Action on the Foreign Affairs Committee of the Democratic Party." Neither audience is likely to be taken with a speech on "What ever happened to the Dodo?"—a topic that might be endlessly fascinating to an audience of physical anthropologists. If you suspect the importance of your speech topic, poll the class members and ask them about it.

The following are examples of trivial topics:

> How frisbees are thrown
>
> Baking a cake at an altitude of 6000 feet
>
> Steps involved in burying a dog
>
> The chemistry of toenail polish
>
> The singing range of parakeets

Intimate topics   Excessive self-confession in a speech is more likely to embarrass than to spellbind an audience. Doubtless, all of us have had intimate experiences and insights that we would dearly love to share. Do so by all means with a friend, a parent, a counselor, a pastor, but not with the audience of your speech class. Personal traumas, tragedies, heartbreaks, and so on, have a limited use as anecdotal asides, but should not be made the principal topic of a speech. Examples of intimate topics that are better left alone are:

> My first sexual experience
>
> The greatest heartbreak I have ever suffered
>
> How I almost killed myself
>
> My experience with Jesus

Criteria for choosing a suitable topic

It is always easier to lay down a series of don't's rather than enunciate a series of do's. In this case, a useful list of do's on topic choice is difficult to catalog. We offer, however, the following general guidelines for selecting a useable topic.

Choose a topic that suits you   Enthusiasms, avocations, preoccupations, and interests vary from one human being to another. We love one thing, hate another, and are lukewarm about a third. This first principle of choosing a speech topic merely advises speakers to select one that reflects their interests. It is easier for speakers to talk about something they know and love, rather than something they scarcely know and hardly care about. This is commonsense advice, perhaps, but it is well worth heeding. If you have to make a speech about a foreign city and have been to London but not to Paris, talk about London. If you love English and loathe science, find an English topic to talk about.

But this advice, of course, cannot be pursued to an absurd and selfish extent; some thought should be given to the wishes and tastes of your audience. If the topic you know best and really want to talk about is a thing esoteric, remote, and alien to your audience, then you must try to find some compromise subject mutually satisfying to both you and your audience. Let us say, for example, that a speaker has an overriding passion for ocean liners, and an especial love for ships of the White Star Company. A lay audience would probably not be interested in a topic such as "The naval career of the White Star liner, *Olympic*"; nor for that matter, in a talk on "Techniques of traverse bulkhead engineering used in the construction of White Star liners." But an audience would most likely be enthralled about hearing a speech on, "Why the White Star liner, the *Titanic,* sank." Similarly, it is the rare student audience that will willingly suffer through a speech on "Why it is bad strategy in Monopoly to buy utilities"; that same audience, however, would probably be more receptive to a speech on "How Monopoly was invented." The idea is to choose a subject that matches your interest and enthusiasms and, at the same time, takes into account the tastes and temperament of your audience.

Choose a topic suitable to the situation　　Nature abhors a vacuum; so should speakers. Sensible speakers pondering the selection of a speech topic should ask themselves these three questions: Why? To whom? and For how long should I speak? The answers to these questions affect the selection of the final topic.

The situation in which student speeches are given is clear-cut and ready-made. As a result students are considerably tempted to accept it at face value and plod on with the first topic that comes to mind. Resist this temptation. A classroom speech topic needs to be as skillfully chosen as the topic for a speech before the United Nations, if only because students bore as easily as delegates. Consider, therefore, as you go about preparing the speech, why you are giving it, to whom, and how long it should be.

The "why" is the most readily answered of these questions. Pragmatically, you are giving the speech to satisfy a class requirement. But you must have some more general purpose in mind, or you are sure to ramble. What effect do you wish the speech to have on the audience? Do you want to arouse them to some cause, inform them on some issue, persuade them to some action, or to have them laughing so hard they are rolling on the floor? Basically, speeches can be classified under three general categories: to inform, to persuade, or to entertain. These categories are not mutually exclusive. A speaker may inform, persuade, and even entertain in a single speech. But it is useful, nevertheless, to conceptualize some general effect that you intend the speech to have, and to bear this in mind not only as you prepare the speech but even before you have chosen the topic.

To whom is the speech to be given? The audience of a classroom speech is curiously dual—made up of many novices and one expert. Your peers in the class make up the novice population; the teacher is the expert. It is, of course, essential that the speech have something in it to please the teacher, who will ultimately grade it. But at the same time, your speech must also satisfy your peers, otherwise they will shuffle, cough, mutter to one another, and be unspeakably bored, all of which will no doubt affect the teacher's evaluation of your speech. Bear in mind, therefore, before you even jot down the first word or think the first thought, that the topic of your speech has got to satisfy this curiously dual audience.

But what do you know about your peers, who make up the majority of your audience? Do you have even the vaguest idea of what they are like? Do you know anything about their political ideas, about their values and backgrounds, indeed, about how they are likely to react to your chosen topic? If the class is small, you can conduct an unofficial poll simply by talking to various class members. Larger classes require more careful study and observation. You need to bear in mind such variables as age, cultural and ethnic composition, sex, and educational level of the class members. For instance, though public speaking is a freshman course, you might find yourself in a class that has a disproportionate number of seniors, requiring you to pitch your speech at a slightly higher level if you wish to hold their interest. Likewise, a sizeable number of the class members might have a group affiliation that could prejudice their response to your speech. For instance, before giving a speech attacking fraternities and sororities, you'd be well advised to find out how many members of the class belong to such organizations. The advice here is not that you blandly cater to your intended audience. If you are a real firebrand when it comes to fraternities and sororities and intend to blast them no matter what, fine, go right ahead. But knowing in advance the number of the opposition in the class will at least give you an inkling of how much ammunition you will need, and how vigorous a counterfire you can expect. All we're saying, along with the Boy Scouts, is: Be prepared.

If all this strikes you as too vague, then create a questionnaire and circulate it among the class. The questionnaire can be used to get basic information about the class members—age, sex, ethnic composition, class standing, group affiliation—factors that invariably affect an audience's response to a speech. You might ask questions about hobbies, interests, academic majors, and career ambitions. If you discover, for instance, that of the thirty-five people in the class, twenty of them are business majors, you can be fairly sure that some business related topic will hold the majority's interest.

The final question you should ask yourself is how long should your speech be. Student speeches are generally restricted to about five minutes, at the end of which time many instructors will promptly interrupt to allow for the next student to give his or her speech. The topic of the speech is necessarily affected by this brief time limit. Student speeches cannot ramble, cannot have unbearably long introductions, and cannot be interspersed with leisurely asides. The speech must be concise, must move rapidly from point to point, and must pack whatever wallop it intends to have within the space of about five hundred words. A five-minute time limit also means that the topic cannot be complex or especially broad. Wars and revolutions cannot be covered in five minutes; the evolution of species or the creation of constellations cannot be intelligently broached in five minutes. Bear in mind, therefore, as you select a topic that five minutes is about the length of time that it takes to read aloud a page and a half from a typical book, and that should be the approximate length of your speech.

THE CENTRAL IDEA

The central idea of a speech—sometimes called the thesis, the specific purpose, or the controlling idea—is an exact statement of what the speech proposes to do. Usually stated early in the speech, the central idea predicts, controls, and obligates the movement of the speech toward a certain direction. Here is an example from a student's speech "Why the White Star liner, the *Titanic,* sank."

On April 14th, 1912, the White Star liner, *Titanic,* billed in the newspapers as "unsinkable," struck an iceberg off the coast of Newfoundland and sank with the loss of 1,513 lives. The disaster has inspired poems, songs, sermons, movies, and books. Why

> did the *Titanic*, a ship thought unsinkable, go down? Two defects in the design of the *Titanic* contributed to the disaster: Her steering was sluggish and unresponsive, even for a ship of her immense size; her traverse bulkheads, which should have made her nearly unsinkable, did not extend all the way up to her deck.

The central idea of the speech—the underlined sentence—promises to answer the question, "Why did the *Titanic* go down?" by elaborating on two causes: her unresponsive steering and her badly designed bulkheads.

The central idea of a speech may also take the form of a statement of purpose, as when a speaker announces:

> The purpose of this speech is to explain to students why cafeteria prices have risen so dramatically over the past two semesters.

Or, for that matter, a central idea may be in the form of a question, which the speech then proceeds to answer, as in the following example:

> Why do ships float—have you ever wondered that? The largest passenger liner of all times, The *Queen Elizabeth*, 83,673 gross tons, 1,031 feet long and 118 feet seven inches wide, sailed the seas serenely for years, yet a tiny three ounce pebble tossed into the water will immediately sink. Why should a massive iron ship float, and a tiny pebble sink?

The central idea, whether in the form of a sentence, a statement of purpose, or a question, serves two primary purposes in a speech. First, it restricts the speaker to a rather specific agenda, thereby discouraging rambling. Once speakers enunciate that they intend to talk on something specific, there is a good likelihood that they will carry through on their promise without irritating digression. Speakers, on the other hand, who begin speeches with only a vague notion of what they intend to talk about, run the risk of endlessly hedge-hopping from one topic to another.

Second, the central idea gives the audience a structure to anticipate, making the speech easier to follow. For instance, the speaker who begins a speech by announcing:

> Two defects in the design of the *Titanic* contributed to the disaster: Her steering was sluggish and unresponsive; her traverse bulkheads, which should have made her virtually unsinkable, did not extend all the way up to her deck.

has informed the audience not only of the main points to be covered, but also of their sequence in the speech. The audience expects to hear first about the unresponsive steering of the *Titanic* and then about her poorly designed bulkheads. Anticipating this structure, the audience is better able to follow the movement of the speech. In effect, a central idea serves as a focusing device for both speaker and audience, making a speech simpler to give and easier to listen to.

Finding the central idea

How is the central idea of a speech arrived at? Methods vary from one speaker to another. One speaker might immediately think of the central idea of a speech even before researching the topic. Another speaker may be through with the research before a central idea comes to mind. A third may have to pore over masses of information and data before the vaguest glimmer of a central idea occurs to him. Thinking up a speech is not as lock step a process as baking a cake.

For those students who have trouble devising a central idea, we offer the following two-step method.

Brainstorm on paper   With pen in hand, find a quiet corner and write down the thoughts that come to mind. If your mind is blank, write down "my mind is blank." Work as quickly as you can, jotting down all your ideas, no matter how unrelated. Perhaps, after five minutes of brainstorming, your list might look like this:

1. I hate doing this.

2. My astrological sign is Pisces.

3. I read an interesting book about the *Titanic*.

4. Movies nowadays are very bad.

5. The cafeteria has raised its food prices again.

6. My mind is completely blank.

7. My eye doctor is an optometrist, but my sister goes to an ophthalmologist.

8. I love my mother, but can't stand her sister.

9. My state has adopted no-fault insurance.

10. Libraries are too quiet.

11. Lawyers are overpaid.

12. Mathematics is my worst subject.

Select the best random thought   The preceding list contains several useful ideas for topics. Select the idea that appeals most to you and ask yourself questions about it. For instance, if on item number three you asked the question, "What caused the *Titanic* disaster?" the answer would generate the central idea given earlier. "Two defects in the design of the *Titanic* contributed to the disaster: Her steering was sluggish and unresponsive, even for a ship of her immense size; her traverse bulkheads, which should have made her nearly unsinkable, did not extend all the way up to her deck." On the other hand, the question: "Who perished with the *Titanic?*" might produce the following central idea: "The survival list of the *Titanic*'s passengers reveals that a strong class bias was at work in determining which passengers were allowed on lifeboats and which were left to drown." The question asked in item number 9, "What is no-fault insurance?" might generate the following central idea: "No-fault insurance is a state law that requires insurance companies to settle personal injury claims of their own clients up to a specific dollar limit without regard to liability or fault." Amplified with appropriate facts, statistics, and examples, this central idea could be the basis for an informative speech about no-fault insurance.

Asking an intelligent question about any of the items on this list doesn't necessarily mean that you'll immediately be able to give an answer. You might have to do considerable research before you can make any sense of the question. Nevertheless, this method of devising a central idea will at least steer you toward a specific and researchable topic.

Five errors to avoid in devising a central idea

1. A central idea must not be expressed as a fragment, but must be a complete sentence.

Poor: Cafeteria food prices very high.

Better: The cafeteria food prices have risen dramatically because the wholesale cost of food has gone up and because the new minimum-wage law has doubled the payroll for student helpers.

2. The central idea must not be vague, wishy-washy, or purposeless.

Poor: Bad things happen to your body when you smoke cigarettes.

Better: Cigarette smoking harms the body by constricting the blood vessels, speeding up the heartbeat, clogging the bronchial tubes, and activating excessive gastric secretions in the stomach.

3. The central idea must not contain two unrelated propositions or arguments.

Poor: I favor the Equal Rights Amendment and also believe that people should not be forced to pay into Social Security if they don't want to.

The central idea, as it presently exists, threatens to split the speech into two irreconcilable topics—the Equal Rights Amendment and the fairness of Social Security. One or the other must be settled on, or the speech will tug hopelessly in two directions.

Better: I favor the Equal Rights Amendment because, depending on the interpretation of the courts, it promises to equalize employment opportunities between men and women.

Better: Social Security should be made elective rather than compulsory because it has proved to be a bad investment for many subscribers, and because its solvency is now seriously in doubt.

4. A central idea must not be expressed in figurative language.

Poor: When it comes to poisons, botulism takes the cake.

Better: Botulism poisoning is caused by an anerobe bacillus whose toxin is the deadliest poison in the world.

5. A central idea must not be expressed in muddled language.

Poor: Homosexuality is a status offense because the participants are willing so that the relationship is voluntary in character rather than the type described in a victim-perpetrator model.

Better: When participants in a homosexual act are consenting adults, then homosexuality should be considered a status rather than a criminal offense.

EXERCISES

1. Which of the following topics would be suitable for an in-class speech?

    a. The day I got my abortion

    b. Matrilineal kinship affiliation systems among the !Kwong bushmen

    c. How children blow bubbles

    d. Famine in the world

    e. The coming impact of cable television

2. Arrange the following topics in descending order from the biggest to the smallest.

    a. Marilyn Monroe movies

    b. Famous comedy teams in the movies

    c. The history of movies

    d. The special effects in *Star Wars*

3. Which of the following topics is too technical for an in-class speech?

    a. The cause of smog

    b. Photochemical reaction of freon on the ozone layer

    c. Carcinogens in the water supply

    d. Seven steps you can take to avoid cancer

4. Which of the following topics is too trivial?

> a. How to give an in-class speech
>
> b. Bathing a canary
>
> c. Why I am an optimist
>
> d. Drug references in pop-music lyrics

5. Which of the following topics is too intimate to be used in an in-class speech?

> a. How to buy a used car
>
> b. The usefulness of lovelorn columns in the newspaper
>
> c. What cereal manufacturers put on their labels
>
> d. The guilt I felt when I left my first wife

6. Your speech class is primarily composed of Liberal Arts majors. Which of the following topics would be the most suitable for such an audience?

> a. Buying preferred stock versus municipal bonds
>
> b. The economic theories of Karl Marx
>
> c. The possibilities of hydrogen as a fuel supply
>
> d. Black comedy in modern movies

7. By an enrollment fluke, 95 percent of your speech class is made up of the college's athletes. Which of the following topics do you think is likely to have the most appeal for them?

> a. Shelley as a revolutionary seer
>
> b. The economic theories of Adolf Hitler
>
> c. Enlarging your vocabulary through the study of antonyms
>
> d. Knee injuries in sports: their frequency and cause

8. Criticize the following central ideas.

> a. How life in the ghetto
>
> b. Woman's Liberation is a nutty movement
>
> c. It was hypothesized that certain physical and demographic data constitute suitable predictor factors in anticipating and evaluating suicide potential among teenagers

9. What is wrong with the following central idea?

> Marie Antoinette was not as bad as everybody makes out plus the guillotine was invented in the eighteenth century as a humanitarian execution method

10. Why would a teacher most likely object to the following central idea?

> Football playing is for the birds

How to use supporting details

A speech has two parts. You must state your thesis, and you must prove it.

—Aristotle

GENERALIZATIONS

A student is giving an in-class speech against the hot dog. Simply stated, the central idea of her speech is that hot dogs are nutritionally worthless. She has done what she thinks is adequate research, assembled her findings into an outline, and is now ready to make the speech. Below is a paragraph from the speech as it was delivered.

> Hot dogs are bad for you. They can make you feel sick. They have a lot of fat and little protein. Many authorities in the field of consumer protection have declared that hot dogs have no nutritional value. They contain a blend of artificial additives and chemicals that have a negative effect on the human physiology. In fact, under the FDA, the quality of hot dogs has gotten worse because hot dog manufacturers are now allowed to put all kinds of foreign substances and fillers in hot dogs, things that aren't good for you. You can get fat from them, while starving your body of badly needed nutrients.

The student went on for another three or four minutes in more or less the same vein, finally concluding with a weak plea that the audience refrain from eating hot dogs. The result of all her persuasions? A politely uninterested audience and a rather poor grade. The instructor stated in an evaluation that the speech was too general and that the student failed to make a specific and substantial enough case against the hot dog.

This student speech suffered from a defect common to many everyday assertions and arguments: excessive vagueness. Everything the student had said was indeed true, and she made no assertion that she hadn't either read or heard somewhere. Her audience, no doubt, had also heard and read something similar about hot dogs. But by failing to support her claims and arguments with specific details, she persuaded no one and communicated little of value.

SPECIFIC DETAILS

An assertion may be generalized or it may be made in specific detail. Because it is easier to rattle off generalizations than to talk in specifics, all of us at one time or another are guilty of blithely generalizing: "Coffee is bad for you"; "Inflation is very high"; "Football players are dumb"; "Blondes have more fun"; "Communists are horrid." The catalog of generalizations that you can hear in the everyday world is literally endless. And while it may be unreasonable to expect casual conversation to be rigorous and exacting, it is certainly not unreasonable for an instructor to expect the assertions of an in-class speech to be made in specific detail. To illustrate how the same assertions can be made in varying degrees of specificity, we have prepared a chart listing alternatives to many of the student's assertions about the hot dog:

I *Vague*	II *Less Vague*	III *Specific*
Hot dogs can make you feel sick.	Hot dogs can give you headaches.	Hot dogs are cured with sodium nitrate, a substance which, according to the American Academy of Neurology, causes headaches in many people.

I	II	III
Vague	*Less Vague*	*Specific*
Hot dogs have a lot of fat and little protein in them.	Hot dogs have about 10 percent protein and 90 percent fat and other substances.	The U.S. Department of Agriculture claims that today's hot dogs are comprised of 29 percent fat, 11.7 percent protein, and 60.3 percent salt, spices, preservatives, and water.
Many authorities in the fields of consumer protection have declared that the hot dog has no nutritional value.	Ralph Nader and other consumer rights advocates agree that hot dogs are nutritionally worthless.	"Hot dogs," says Ralph Nader, "are among America's deadliest missiles"; New York City's Consumer Affairs Commissioner Bess Myerson agrees: "After I found out what was in hot dogs," she says, "I stopped eating them."

The assertions made in any public speech should be supported by the sort of specific details found in column III. Generalizations, of course, have their place; one cannot give a speech filled entirely with details without becoming excessively technical and boring. But whenever a notion or idea is presented that is crucial to the central contention of your speech, you should hasten to support it with as many details as you can possibly muster.

SUPPORT GENERALIZATIONS WITH SPECIFIC DETAILS

The various kinds of details that can be advanced in support of any idea or claim include: facts, definitions, examples, testimonials, statistics, anecdotes, and diagrams.

Facts

A fact is an assertion about reality. The assertion is a fact if it accurately represents reality and if it is verifiable. The first condition simply says that to be a fact, an assertion about anything must be true; the second condition demands that this truth be the same for any two people.

Consider, for instance, the following assertion about hot dogs: "Federal law permits manufacturers to include the esophagi, lips, snouts, ears, and skeletal muscle tissue of cattle in hot dogs." This statement qualifies as a fact because it is both true and verifiable. Federal law does indeed permit the inclusion of such suspect edibles in hot dogs; moreover, the existence of such a law can be verified by anyone who reads the statute books. By the same reasoning, however, a statement such as "Astrological forces influence the performance of the stock market" must be regarded as a statement of belief rather than an assertion of fact since the effects of astrology have never been adequately verified.

Facts add a convincing ring to any speech. The speaker who makes a vague assertion such as "The FDA allows manufacturers to put all kinds of foreign substances in hot dogs" sounds fuzzy, uncertain, and inept. Better, and by far more convincing, to word the assertion more specifically, saying something like this: "Manufacturers, with the blessings of the FDA, add to their hot dogs a variety of chemicals such as sodium nitrite, sodium acid pyrophosphate, and delta lactone—whose effects on the human physiology are so far unknown. Without such additives, hot dogs would lose their fluffy texture and robust pink color, and begin to look like the flabby, chewey, unappetizing scraps of meat and gristle that they really are."

Sources for facts   The reference section of a library is the best source of facts available to the student speaker. Encyclopedias found there provide excellent summaries of state-of-the-art facts on a variety of subjects. Reference volumes of various kinds, including the indexes and abstracts on different subjects, are also prime sources for facts. (See Chapter 6.)

Definitions

A definition is a statement of what a thing is or of what a term or concept means. Experienced speakers, who give speeches on complex topics, usually begin by defining all crucial abstract terms. Here, for example, in a speech entitled "Why I Am an Agnostic," delivered at a religious symposium in 1929, the famed trial lawyer Clarence Darrow begins by saying what he means by *agnostic:*

> An agnostic is a doubter. The word is generally applied to those who doubt the verity of accepted religious creeds of faith. Everyone is an agnostic as to the beliefs and creeds they do not accept. Catholics are agnostic to the Protestant creeds, and the Protestants are agnostic to the Catholic creed. Anyone who thinks is an agnostic about something, otherwise he must believe that he is possessed of all knowledge. And the proper place for such a person is in the madhouse or the home for the feeble-minded. In a popular way, in the western world, an agnostic is one who doubts or disbelieves the main tenets of the Christian faith.

Because abstract terms symbolize ideas, notions, or concepts that can be variously interpreted by different listeners, it is especially necessary for speakers to define all such terms in the speech. The student giving a speech on a topic such as "The Role of Love in Modern Marriages" should begin by defining *love* since it is a term fuzzy and abstract enough to trigger off many contradictory interpretations in an audience. (For a full discussion of *abstract* and *concrete* terms, see Chapter 9.)

Sources for definitions   An obvious and useful source for definitions of terms is the dictionary, in all its various forms. Some dictionaries define the formal words of standard English; others catalog the origins of various slang terms such as "hot dog." For instance, the *Dictionary of Word and Phrase Origins* by William and Mary Morris lists the following explanation for the origins of *hot dog:*

> The first recorded appearance in print of the term "hot dog" is in 1903. The late Henry L. Mencken, as would be expected by anyone familiar with his massive and enormously entertaining tome, *The American Language,* did some very thorough research on the origins of "hot dog." His findings: although sausages in rolls have been sold in this country for many years, the first person to heat the roll and add mustard and relish was Harry Stevens, concessionaire at the Polo Grounds, home of the New York Giants. And the coiner of the name "hot dog"? None other than the late T. A. Dorgan, who, signing his work "Tad," was undoubtedly the best-known sports cartoonist of the era.

Assuredly not essential information but interesting and curious enough to have added spice to an otherwise dull speech—if the student had used it.

Examples

Examples can be used to provide a listener with a specific application of a general idea or principle. Without examples, assertions tend to sound vague and unconvincing; illustrated with adequate examples, even the most far-fetched assertion can be made to sound probable. Here is an example:

> Jonah could have been swallowed whole by a sperm whale. . . . A ship in the South Seas in 1771 had one of her boats bitten in two by a sperm whale. The beast seized one unlucky crew member in her mouth and went down with him. On returning to the surface the whale ejected him on the wreckage of the broken boat, much bruised but not seriously injured. . . . A worse fate befell another victim in 1891. The *Star of the East* was in the vicinity of the Falkland Islands and the lookout sighted a large sperm whale three miles away. Two boats were launched and in a short time one of the harpooners was enabled to spear the fish. The second boat attacked the whale but was upset by a lash of its tail and the men thrown into the sea, one man being drowned, and another, James Bartley, having disappeared, could not be found. The whale was killed and *in a few hours* was lying by the ship's side and the crew were busy with axes and spades removing the blubber. *They worked all day and part of the night.* Next morning they attached some tackle to the stomach which was hoisted on the deck. The sailors were startled by something in it which gave spasmodic signs of life, and inside was found the missing sailor, doubled up and unconscious. He was laid on the deck and treated to a bath of sea water which soon revived him.[1]

Examples should not replace facts, but merely supplement them. Nothing is more frustrating to listen to than a dreary and silly recital of specific examples that prove nothing. For instance, a favorite ploy of some people in arguing against the welfare system is to cite case after case of some chiselers they heard about who eat steak and drive Cadillacs—all on the weekly dole. No doubt such cases do exist here and there, but citing examples of them does not prove that a majority of welfare recipients cheat, which is usually the underlying contention of this argument. "Hasty generalization" is the term logicians use to characterize this error in reasoning of drawing sweeping conclusions from one or two examples.

Examples alone merely establish the probability of an assertion, but they do not prove it. Because one sailor was swallowed by a sperm whale in 1771, and another in 1891 does not prove that Jonah was similarly engulfed. The examples merely indicate that something similar *could* have happened to Jonah. Assertions supported by examples alone should be cautiously worded to imply not proof, but probability.

Sources for examples   These are more varied than the sources of cut and dried facts. You might find, for instance, rather supportive examples from the experiences of your own friends. If you were giving a speech about the inefficiency of federal bureaucracy, you might cite the instance of an elderly acquaintance who has been badly mishandled by some office of the federal government. Perhaps you might even find an example from your own experiences to demonstrate this inefficiency. Beware, however, of building an argument on examples alone, or of making sweeping generalizations based on the recital of one or two instances.

Testimonials

The testimonial is a statement that cites the views, opinions, or experiences of someone else. Sometimes referred to as "witness evidence," or "authority opinion," testimonials, like examples, should be used to support rather than to replace hard facts. In citing testimonials, speakers are, in essence, trying to marshal favorable and supportive opinions behind their causes. The quality of the testimonial will consequently vary with the reputation and credentials of the person being quoted. Testimonials should be brief and to the point. Long, rambling testimonials will bore an audience.

Ordinarily, if the testimonial is from an authority, the authority should first be named and his or her credentials summarized before the opinion is quoted or paraphrased. Here is an example, taken from a speech decrying the quality of inner city schools:

> John Goodlad, dean of the UCLA College of Education, concluded that the schools are "anything but the palaces of an affluent society." On the contrary, he writes, "They look more like the artifacts of a society that did not really care about its schools, a society that expressed its disregard by creating schools less suited to human habitation than its prisons."

The reason for such an introduction is obvious: to lend the authority's prestige to the testimonial.

If the persons being quoted are well known, then it is unnecessary to mention their credentials. Here is an example:

> When Harry Truman was asked about a President's power, he said that, "The biggest power the President has . . . is the power to persuade people to do what they ought to do without having to be persuaded. And if a man thinks he's too big to do the necessary persuading, then he's in for trouble, and so is the country."

On the other hand, where unknown persons are being quoted because of some rare experience they have had, the introduction should specify enough about them to make their testimonials credible. Here is an example:

> Delsey Cortez of Albuquerque, New Mexico, was a state trooper for five years. Her record indicated that she was a stable and honest person. She sighted a UFO on one of her patrols. She described the spaceship as "taking off straight up" with a deafening roar.

Always bear in mind that the purpose of the introduction is simply to make the testimonial persuasive and intelligible. Long-winded introductions are usually unnecessary.

A testimonial may also be cited in paraphrase, rather than in an actual quotation. Here is an example:

> In every major city of the world our air is full of smoke and smog. When the Apollo 10 astronauts flew over Los Angeles, they still saw a yellow smudge even though they were about twenty-five thousand miles up.

Sources for testimonials   Testimonials can be gathered from a variety of sources. The opinions of various experts can be easily extracted from books and articles. (See Bibliography, p. 90.) Local authorities to whom you have access—such as doctors, teachers, and other professionals—can be interviewed for testimonials on their subject of expertise. The opinions of friends and acquaintances who have either a rare experience to share or an unusual expertise in some field can also be cited. You should not use the testimony of any person whose truthfulness is suspect or whose credentials are bogus.

Statistics

The word *statistics* comes from German, where it originally meant the materials that made up the political strength of a state. First used in English in the title "A Statistical Account of Scotland"—a volume published by Sir John Sinclair in 1791—*statistics* now refers to facts and data classified and expressed in numbers.

Though statistics are especially useful in depicting the nature of large groups or collections, inexperienced speakers should nevertheless use them cautiously in their speeches. Nothing numbs an audience more quickly than a boring recital of statistics, especially statistics that describe a complicated relationship between two groups. Moreover, audiences of all kinds are traditionally suspicious of speakers who are too glib with statistics.

Used sparingly, however, statistics can add a convincing precision to any speech. For instance, a speaker could say something like this to an audience:

Some examples of resource use and environmental impact are seen in the following statements:

1. We are presently destroying massive acreages of land each year.

2. We throw away, use, and discharge every year into our environment:
   a. Mountains of cans
   b. Untold numbers of bottles
   c. Enough smoke to blanket the Plains States
   d. Enough carbon monoxide to kill millions
   e. A vast amount of hydrocarbon gas
   f. An incredible number of junked automobiles
   g. Huge amounts of nitrogen oxide
   h. Tons and tons of lead.

We use more oil, natural gas, coal, and other kinds of energy than any other country in the world.[2]

Or, the same statements could be made more statistically:

Some examples of resource use and environmental impact are seen in the following statements:

1. We are currently destroying agricultural land at the rate of 1,000,000 acres per year.

2. We discard, use, or discharge into the environment each year:
   a. 48,000,000,000 cans
   b. 26,000,000,000 bottles
   c.   142,000,000 tons of smoke
   d.   61,000,000 tons of carbon monoxide
   e.   16,000,000 tons of hydrocarbon gases
   f.   7,000,000 junked automobiles
   g.   6,000,000 tons of nitrogen oxide
   h.   210,000 tons of lead

We use each day 4 gallons of oil, 300 cubic feet of natural gas, 15 pounds of coal, and smaller amounts of energy from other sources per person—eight times the world average.

It is obvious which version is the more convincing.

The statistics recited above are easy to follow because they are grouped in succession to depict a single phenomenon: waste. Other kinds of statistics, especially comparative statistics, are more difficult to follow. The passage below—from a speech given by an Assistant Secretary of Education—uses statistics in a way that must have come close—one suspects—to boggling the audience:

I received just before I left for Kansas a report from the National Center for Education Statistics which will be sent to the President showing that the salaries of women relative to men have not significantly improved either in private or public institutions of higher education. Women's salaries were 82.9 percent of men's salaries in 1972, and they were 83.2 percent in 1974. Women were also disadvantaged in the tenure situation where 26.7 percent of the women and 57 percent of the men had tenure. In academic rank, for example, in 1972 the total number of full women Professors was 9.8 percent and in 1974, 10.3 percent; women Associate Professors in 1972 numbered 16.3 percent and in 1974, 27.1 percent. The complete survey will be published at a later date, and I'd be very happy to send it to you.[3]

Common sense dictates some cautions in the use of statistics in a speech. First, you should not use statistics so excessively as to bore an audience. Second, statistics should not be used to illustrate trivial points. For instance, in a speech about the composition of hot dogs, it would obviously be silly to rattle off precise numbers about the amount of mustard annually used on hot dogs. Finally, all statistics quoted should be either preceded or followed by an explanation of their significance. Here is an example:

> The increasing size of the metropolitan area is compounding the problems local authorities must face. Since 1940, our population has grown by 50,000,000, the use of energy has quadrupled, disposable income has increased by 60%—yet—our air supply remains the same. In such a setting air pollution is murder.

Sources for statistics   You should mention where your statistics came from, unless they were derived from an obviously verifiable source. The statistics quoted above, for instance, are taken from census figures, which can easily be checked. But if you got your figures from some obscure or unpublished source, you should name it. Doing so gives any skeptics in your audience a chance to verify your figures.

Anecdotes

An anecdote is a brief story or episode, often humorous, that is told to add dramatic impact to an idea or proposition. Frequently, speakers will use anecdotes as a lead-in to more serious topics. Here is an example of an anecdote used by a speaker just before he began a recital of some statistics:

> I never listen to a speaker launch out on one of those long discussions, filled with statistics of all kinds, or commit the same error myself, but that I think of the professor in a western university who taught mathematics and statistics. One day he was swimming, dressed in his bathing suit, at the edge of a swimming pool on the university campus when a beautiful coed accidentally dropped her camera into the deep end of the pool. She called to the elderly professor for help. He said he would be

glad to dive down after the camera, but first wanted to know why she happened to choose him when there were so many young men within easy reach to do the job. She answered, "Professor, you have apparently forgotten me, but I am in your large statistics class. I have found that you can *go down deeper, stay down longer, and come up drier* than anyone I know."—I do not propose to go down too deep, stay down too long, or come up too dry with these statistics.

Anecdotes, of course, do not prove a speaker's point, but merely enliven it. Here, for instance, in his second address on energy, delivered over nationwide television on November 8, 1977, President Carter relates an anecdote:

A few weeks ago in Detroit an unemployed steelworker told me something that may reflect the feelings of many of you. "Mr. President," he said, "I don't feel much like talking about energy and foreign policy. I am concerned about how I'm going to live. I can't be too concerned about other things when I have a 10-year-old daughter to raise and I don't have a job, and I'm 56 years old."

Well, I understand how he felt, but I must tell you the truth, and the truth is that you cannot talk about our economic problems now or in the future without talking about energy.

This anecdote added a poignant, human touch to the speech.

Overuse of anecdotal material can give a speech a frivolous, folksy tone unsuitable to serious topics. Inexperienced speakers should therefore be especially careful in their use of anecdotes.

Diagrams and other graphics

In short speeches, such as are usually given in speech classes, diagrams often belabor the point, adding clutter rather than clarity to a presentation. Where the speech is long and the subject complicated, diagrams are useful, but such speeches are rarely given to fulfill the assignments of a speech class. It is possible, however, for a student to use a diagram in a short speech, especially a diagram that visually dramatizes a significant point. Here, for instance, is a diagram showing the composition of a typical "all meat" frankfurter, which the student who gave the speech on "hot dogs" might have used. The diagram simply reinforces what the student intended to put into words—that hot dogs are made up primarily of fat and water.

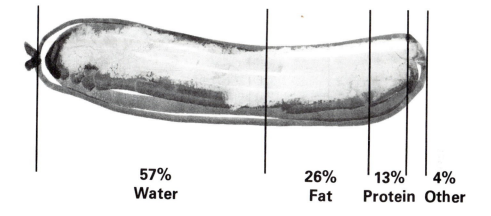

57%
Water

26%
Fat

13%
Protein

4%
Other

Diagrams have to be adapted for use before an audience. The preceding diagram, for instance, is simply too small for the student to have cut out and displayed. Rather, she would have had to transfer the drawing onto a large poster, which could then be hung in front of the blackboard or displayed at an appropriate moment during the speech.

Some commonsense rules should govern your use of diagrams and other graphics. First, diagrams or graphics used to illustrate a point should be instantly and visually clear. It simply doesn't make sense to bring out an elaborate diagram or chart that you will then have to spend ten minutes explaining. Second, diagrams or graphics should illustrate the main point of a speech, not some minor or secondary issue. Granted that preservatives are used in hot dogs, it would nevertheless have been silly of the student who gave the speech on hot dogs to have prepared a chart illustrating the chemical action of preservatives. Third, diagrams should not introduce or explicate any issue not covered directly in the speech. For instance, although much of the blame for the adulteration of frankfurters may be placed on the FDA, it would have been a pointless intrusion for the student to have shown a chart depicting the organizational structure of the FDA bureaucracy. Such a chart belongs in another speech.

MODEL SPEECH

The use of supporting details is illustrated in the following speech. Since the speech uses no crucial abstract terms that need to be defined, no definitions are given. The model does, however, illustrate the use of facts, testimonials, statistics, example, diagram, and anecdote.

Model speech illustrating the use of supporting detail.

HOT DOGS AND COLD FACTS

Anecdote

A fifty-eight-year old man suffering from recurring headaches goes from doctor to doctor but gets no relief. Finally, his condition is diagnosed at the University of California's Dept. of Neurology: The patient is suffering from "hot-dog headaches." What on earth, you ask, are hot-dog headaches? Simple: They're headaches suffered by people who eat hot dogs and are sensitive to sodium nitrite. For the hot dog has sodium nitrite in it. In fact, the hot dog is so adulterated with chemicals, so contaminated with bacteria, so puffy with gristle, fat, water, and so lacking in protein, that it is nutritionally worthless.

Central idea of speech predicts its organization.

First generalization

The chemical content of the hot dog might possibly account for the dog's vague resemblence to a test tube.

Facts

Chemicals such as sodium nitrite, sodium acid pyrophosphate, and glucona delta lactone are added to hot dogs to keep them looking fresh and pink and to make their meat firm and chewy.

Testimonial

"Children," says *Consumer Reports*, "have been poisoned by the nitrite consumed in hot dogs." Nitrites have caused cancer in laboratory animals and are suspected carcinogens in humans. While the FDA is investigating, manufacturers are allowed to add sodium nitrite to hot dogs.

Second generalization

But all the chemicals added to hot dogs still haven't made them pure.

Example

For example, in tests conducted on hot dogs by *Consumer Reports*, only two brands tested were below the maximum allowable level of contamination—10,000 bacteria per gram of meat. Forty percent of the samples analyzed—and all national brands were tested—had already begun to spoil, although they had come straight off the shelves and were air shipped under refrigeration to the lab. Rodent hairs and insect parts were also found in all the samples.

Third generalization { The composition of the so called "all meat" hot dog is another gristly story. Federal law permits manufacturers

Facts { to use the hearts, lungs, lips, ears, snouts, and esophagi of cows, goats, and pigs in hot dogs. (Get the idea why it's called "dog"?) In 1970, this ruling was modified to allow

Diagram { the inclusion of chicken skin and meat. Here's what a typical hot dog looks like: (shows diagram) 57 percent water, 26 percent fat, 13 percent protein, and 4 percent other.

Final generalization { The alleged protein content of hot dogs is a joke, an expensive joke. In 1937, the typical hot dog was 19.6 percent protein. Today, according to *Consumer Reports,* the

Statistics { hot dog barely averages 11.7 percent protein. The cost of the protein found in hot dogs when averaged by the price of hot dogs comes to an unbelievable $15 per pound. For that kind of money, you can buy nearly three pounds of filet mignon.

Conclusion { In sum, the hot dog is such a ghastly blend of chemicals, bacteria, gristle, fat, water, insect parts, and rodent

Testimonial { hair that it is nutritionally worthless. "Hot dogs," says Ralph Nader, "are among America's most potent missiles." "After I found out what was in hot dogs," says New York City's Consumer Affairs Commissioner Bess Myerson, "I stopped eating them." Now that you know how nutritionally worthless hot dogs are, so should you.

MODEL SPEECH BIBLIOGRAPHY

"All American Hot Dog Is on Fire." *Life,* 30 June 1972, p. 48.

"Chickening Out on the Frankfurter." *Consumer Reports,* Jan. 1970, pp. 31–33.

"Decline and Fill of the American Hot Dog." *Time,* 2 October 1972, p. 86.

Nader, Ralph. "Don't Eat That Dog." *New Republic,* 18 March 1972, pp. 12–13.

"Frankfurters." *Consumer Reports,* Feb. 1972, pp. 73–79.

"Headaches from Hot Dogs?" *Science Digest,* Aug. 1972, p. 85.

"Some People Are Getting Headaches from Eating Hot Dogs." *National Observer,* 27 May 1972, p. 9.

EXERCISES

1. Align the statements within each group of assertions in order of specificity, from the most general to the most specific:

   a. The *Titanic* was the biggest ship of her day.

   b. The *Titanic* was 882.5 feet long and 92.5 feet in extreme breadth.

   c. The *Titanic* was a big ship.

   d. Boswell wrote a biography, *The Life of Johnson,* which is considered a classic of the genre.

   e. Boswell wrote a book.

   f. Boswell wrote a biography.

   g. Love and marriage are traceable back through millions of years of human evolution.

   h. Love and marriage have been around for a long time.

   i. Love and marriage are the products of 35 million years of human evolution.

   j. In October 1957, a sunspot count revealed 263. One sunspot was observed for 200 days, from June to December.

   k. In the fall a few years ago, scientists noticed a lot of sunspots. One lasted a long time.

   l. Twenty years ago, scientists counted over 200 sunspots. One sunspot was observed for over a half a year.

   m. People have lived at as high an altitude as 21,200 feet.

   n. The Tibetan herders live in the settlement of Barudusk-sum, 21,200 feet above sea level.

   o. Some people have been known to live at very high altitudes.

   p. During its best year, the total worldwide sales of General Motors reached a staggering sum.

   q. In 1975, General Motors' sales worldwide were over $34 billion.

   r. During its peak year of 1975, General Motors' worldwide sales totalled $35,724,911,215.

   s. The silly feats people will do for publicity are astonishing. One man, for instance, got his name into the *Guinness Book of Records* by devouring an enormous number of franks in a remarkably short time.

   t. The silly feats people will do for publicity are astonishing. One man, for instance, got his name into the *Guinness Book of Records* by devouring 20 franks in less than 4 minutes.

u. The silly feats people will do for publicity are astonishing. One man, for instance, got his name into the *Guinness Book of Records* by devouring 20 2-oz. franks in 3 minutes, 33 seconds on March 3, 1976.

2. Identify the kinds of supporting detail used in the following assertions.

a. Chemistry is that branch of science which has the task of investigating the materials out of which the universe is made. . . . Chemistry is concerned not only with the composition of . . . substances, but also with their inner structure.

b. At the turn of the century, infectious diseases were the primary health menace to this nation. Acute respiratory conditions such as pneumonia and influenza were the major killers. Tuberculosis, too, drained the nation's vitality. Gastrointestinal infections decimated the child population.

c. People can reduce and lose weight. Alfred Hitchcock went from 365 lbs. to a weight of 200 lbs. Jackie Gleason scaled down from 280 lbs. to 221 lbs.

d. While the professional man is engaged in the struggle for professional success, his wife finds herself in what Betty Friedan calls "the sexual ghetto," with no one to talk to over three-feet tall.

e. The culture gap can also be applied to the school curriculum. In an inner-city parochial school, an old Catholic nun—in all the pomp and circumstance of theological education—spent the entire semester grinding her definition of God into the minds of her third-grade class. "God is a Supreme Being," she said over and over. "God is a Supreme Being." One day she decided to test the results of her efforts. "Tommy," she said, "tell us who God is." And Tommy stood up and very proudly announced, "God is a Green Bean."

f. Divorce rates have been rising in all Western countries. In many countries the rates are rising even faster than in the United States. In 1910 the divorce rate for the United States was 87 per 1000 marriages. In 1965 the rate had risen to an estimated figure of well over 300 per 1000 in many parts of the country.

NOTES

[1]Victor B. Scheffer, *The Year of the Whale* (New York: Scribner's, 1969).

[2]Arthur H. Doerr, "The Bounds of Earth," speech given before Pensacola Home Builders Association, Pensacola, Florida, 6 December 1973.

[3]Virginia Y. Trotter, speech given to the Academic Women Conference, Kansas State University, 15 February 1975.

CHAPTER

Gathering materials

The materials of action are variable, but the use we make of them should be constant.

—Epictetus

USING THE LIBRARY

The library will be the principal source for supporting details on your topic. The information stored in the library is scattered throughout books, newspapers, magazines, journals, and microforms. To do research in the library, therefore, you need to know and understand the systems that libraries use for retrieving stored information and data.

The card catalog

Basic research begins with a search of the card catalog, which literally puts a wealth of information at your fingertips. The card catalog is an alphabetical index of all the books and periodicals in the library. Consisting of 3×5 cards that are stored in drawers, the catalog lists all books under at least three headings on separate cards: author, title, and subject. A book that straddles two or more subjects will be listed separately under each subject. If an editor, translator, or illustrator is involved, the book will also be listed under the name of each in addition to its listing under the name of the author. A book with more than one author is also likely to be listed under the name of each author. On the following pages are examples of three index cards that separately list the same book.

811
San

The complete poems of Carl Sandburg

Sandburg, Carl, 1878–1967.
The complete poems of Carl Sandburg. Rev. and expanded ed. New York, Harcourt Brace Jovanovich [1970]

xxxi, 797 p. 24 cm.

PS3537.A618   1970
ISBN 0–15–120773–9

Library of Congress

811′.5′2

70 [2]

76–78865
MARC

TITLE CARD

811
San

Poetry -- Collections

Sandburg, Carl, 1878–1967.
The complete poems of Carl Sandburg. Rev. and expanded ed. New York, Harcourt Brace Jovanovich [1970]

xxxi, 797 p. 24 cm.

PS3537.A618   1970
ISBN 0–15–120773–9

Library of Congress

811′.5′2

70 [2]

76–78865
MARC

SUBJECT CARD

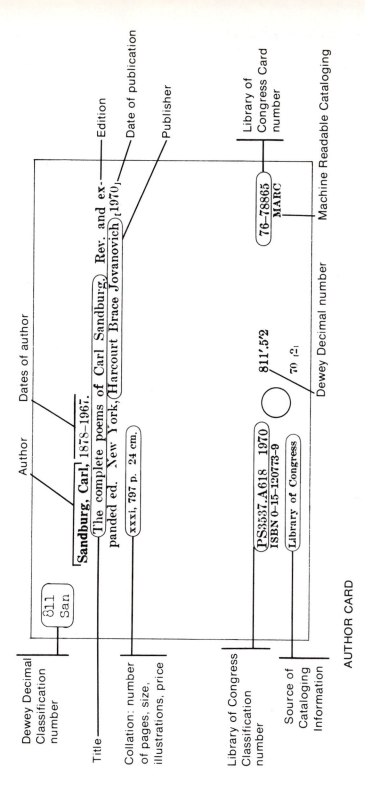

Dewey Decimal Classification number

Author

Dates of author

Title

Collation: number of pages, size, illustrations, price

Library of Congress Classification number

Source of Cataloging Information

Edition

Date of publication

Publisher

Library of Congress Card number

Machine Readable Cataloging

Dewey Decimal number

811
San

Sandburg, Carl, 1878–1967.
The complete poems of Carl Sandburg. Rev. and expanded ed. New York, Harcourt Brace Jovanovich [1970]
xxxi, 797 p. 24 cm.

PS3537.A618 1970
ISBN 0-15-120773-9

Library of Congress

811'.5'2

70 [2]

76–78865
MARC

AUTHOR CARD

Classification of books

Books are filed either under the Dewey Decimal system or the Library of Congress system and stored on shelves called *stacks*. Large libraries often do not allow students to wander in the stacks. Instead, admission is restricted to library employees who will fetch any requested title. Most libraries put out a flyer that explains the classification system used. If you do not understand the system, ask your librarian for help.

Classification of periodicals

Periodicals and newspapers are classified differently from books. Current issues are usually shelved alphabetically by title and are accessible to the public. Back issues, either bound in book form or reproduced on microfilm, are stored elsewhere—usually in a special section of the library. Depending on whether the stacks are open or closed, the public may or may not be admitted.

Classification of nonbooks

Nonbook materials—films, microfilms, recordings, newsclippings, sheet music, reproductions of works of art, transparencies, slides, programmed books, and other similar materials may be listed either in the general catalog or as a special collection. No hard and fast rule exists for classifying this kind of material, so you must ask your library staff which method the library uses.

The references

The reference section is the nerve-center of the library. Reference books systematically list and sum up the information to be found on specific topics. The experienced reseacher, therefore, usually begins a search for information by consulting first the card catalog, and then the general references.

General references index information available on a variety of subjects; specialized references index information on specific subjects. Listed on the following pages are the best-known general references.

Books listing other books

Publishers' Trade List Annual. New York: Bowker, 1873–present. Includes publishers' catalogs, alphabetically arranged. Two important indexes accompany this book: *Books in Print: An Author-Title Series Index* and *Subject Guide to Books in Print: A Subject Index.* Both indexes are published annually. Useful for checking if a book is still on the market. A facsimile page from *Books in Print* is given below.

Name of author in alphabetical order

Title of book

Copyright year

Cross reference to another author

International Standard Bibliographic Number

Price of book

Publisher

Joint author entry

Library of Congress Card Number

Abbot, Morris W. Cog Railway to Pike's Peak. (Illus.). pap. 1.95 (ISBN 0-87095-052-5). Golden West.

Abbot, P. Algebra. (Teach Yourself Ser.). 1974. pap. 2.95 (ISBN 0-679-10386-4). McKay.

Abbot, W. Panama & the Canal. (Panama Ser). 1976. lib. bdg. 34.95. Gordon Pr.

Abbot, W. Robert. Write Me a Verbal Contract. (Illus.). 1961. 8.95 (ISBN 0-87215-001-1). Michie.

Abbot, W. W. The Colonial Origins of the United States, 1607-1763. LC 74-28127. (American Republic Ser). 1975. text ed. 11.00 (ISBN 0-471-00139-2); pap. text ed. 6.00 (ISBN 0-471-00140-6). Wiley.

--Royal Governors of Georgia, 1754-1775. (Institute of Early American History & Culture Ser.). 1959. 7.50x (ISBN 0-8078-0758-3). U of NC Pr.

Abbot, Wilbur C. Bibliography of Oliver Cromwell. 1929. Repr. 23.45. Norwood Edns.

Abbot, Willis J. Watching the World Go by. (American Newspapermen 1790-1933 Ser.). (Illus.). 1974. 16.00 (ISBN 0-8464-0033-2). Beekman Pubs.

Abbott, A. F. Ordinary Level Physics. 1969. pap. text ed. 8.00 (ISBN 0-435-67002-6). Heinemann Ed.

Abbott, A. F. & Nelkon, M. Elementary Physics. Sayer, Michael, ed. (gr. 9-10). 1971. 4.40 ea.; Pt. 1. pap. (ISBN 0-435-67654-7); Pt. 2. pap. (ISBN 0-435-67655-5); pap. text ed. 6.90 combined ed. (ISBN 0-435-67656-3). Heinemann Ed.

Abbott, A. L. Fun Trips in Southern California. pap. 2.95. Main Street.

--Nevada Ghost Towm Trails. (Illus.). pap. 2.95. Main Street.

--Old Bottles: How & Where to Find Them. (Illus.). pap. 2.95. Main Street.

Abbott, Abbe, jt. auth. see Green, Paul.

Abbott, Agatin T., jt. auth. see Macdonald, Gordon A.

Abbott, Allen O. Prison Life in the South: At Richmond, Macon, Savannah, Charleston, Columbia, Charlotte, Raleigh, Goldsboro, & Andersonville During the Years 1864 & 1865. 1976. Repr. of 1866 ed. 25.00 (ISBN 0-403-05657-8, Regency). Scholarly.

Abbott, Andrew. Key to a Better Memory. pap. 1.00. Key Bks.

--Key to Character Reading. pap. 1.00. Key Bks.

Abbott, Anita C. Nature & Human Nature. 1975. pap. 3.00. Valkyrie Pr.

--Shakespearian Grammar. 1870. Repr. 19.75. R West.

Abbott, E. C. We Pointed Them North. 1976. pap. 3.50 (ISBN 0-8061-1366-9). U of Okla Pr.

Abbott, E. C. & Smith, Helena H. We Pointed Them North: Recollections of a Cowpuncher. (Illus.). 1972. Repr. of 1955 ed. 6.95 (ISBN 0-8061-0327-2). U of Okla Pr.

Abbott, Earl L. & Solomon, Erwin S., eds. Instructions for Virginia & West Virginia, 2 vols. 2nd ed. 1962. with 1976 suppl. 75.00 (ISBN 0-87215-077-1); 1976 suppl. 25.00. Michie.

Abbott, Edith. Historical Aspects of the Immigration Problem: Select Documents. LC 69-18753. (American Immigration Collection Ser., No. 1). 1969. Repr. of 1926 ed. 27.00 (ISBN 0-405-00502-4). Arno.

--Immigration: Select Documents & Case Records. LC 69-18754. (American Immigration Collection Ser., No. 1). 1969. Repr. of 1924 ed. 24.00 (ISBN 0-405-00501-6). Arno.

--Public Assistance: American Principles & Policies, 2 Vols. LC 66-13218. 1966. Repr. of 1940 ed. Set. 22.50 (ISBN 0-8462-0736-2). Russell.

--Some American Pioneers in American Social Welfare. (Midway Reprint Ser). 1975. pap. 8.75x (ISBN 0-226-00072-9). U of Chicago Pr.

--Tenements of Chicago, 1908-1935. LC 78-112535. (Rise of Urban America). (Illus.). 1970. Repr. of 1936 ed. lib. bdg. 28.00 (ISBN 0-405-02431-2). Arno.

--Women in Industry: A Study in American Economic History. LC 70-89714. (American Labor, from Conspiracy to Collective Bargaining Ser.: No. 1). 1969. Repr. of 1910 ed. lib. bdg. 17.50 (ISBN 0-405-02101-1). Arno.

--Women in Industry: A Study in American Economic History. 1970. Repr. 14.25 (ISBN 0-442-81084-9). Hacker.

Abbott, Edith & Breckinridge, S. P. The Family & Social Service in the 1920's. LC 74-169361. (Family in America Ser). 1972. 16.00 (ISBN 0-405-03885-2). Arno.

Abbott, Edith & Breckinridge, Sophonisba P. Truancy & Non-Attendance in the Chicago Schools: A Study of the Social Aspects of the Compulsory Education & Child Labor Legislation of Illinois. LC 74-312526. (Rise of Urban America). 1970. Repr. of 1917 ed. lib. bdg. 20.00 (ISBN 0-405-02432-0). Arno.

Sample entries from the author guide to *Books In Print.*

Paperbound Books in Print. New York: Bowker, 1960–present. Monthly record of paperback books. Contains a cumulative index. Listed here are all paperbacks in print.

Books listing book reviews   Books that list book reviews are useful guides whose entries frequently synopsize information about a reviewed book. If you want, for instance, to get the gist of a certain book but don't want to go to the trouble of reading it, check the *Book Review Index* and read what the reviewer had to say about the book.

Book Review Digest. New York: Wilson, 1905–present. Lists reviews from all major American and English periodicals. Published monthly except February and July, with annual cumulations. See the facsimile page from the *Book Review Digest* on page 85.

Book Review Index. Detroit, Michigan: Gale Research Co., 1965–68, 1972–present. Lists reviews appearing in all periodicals of general circulation.

Indexes of periodicals and newspapers   These indexes alphabetically list topics of magazine and newspaper articles, giving title of magazine or newspaper where the article occurred and page number.

Poole's Index to Periodical Literature. 1802–1907. 7 vols. Boston, Mass.: Houghton Mifflin, 1882–1907. This pioneer work indexes close to 600,000 articles in American and English periodicals. Contains a subject index only.

Reader's Guide to Periodical Literature. 1900–present. New York: Wilson, 1905–present. Published semimonthly (monthly in July and August) with quarterly and annual cumulations, this is by far the most popular periodical index, and has been widely used to research sources for thousands of freshman and graduate papers and speeches. Contains an author, subject, and title index to about 160 notable magazines in various fields. See a facsimile on page 86.

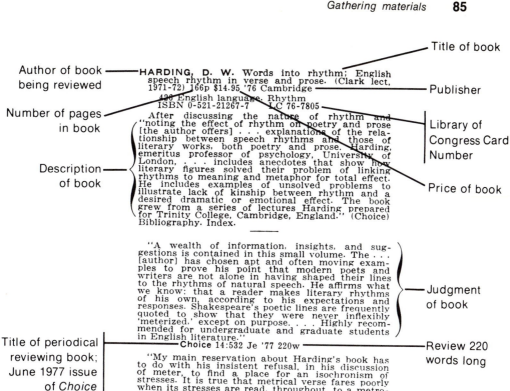

Title of book

Author of book being reviewed

HARDING, D. W. Words into rhythm; English speech rhythm in verse and prose. (Clark lect. 1971-72) 166p $14.95 '76 Cambridge

Publisher

Number of pages in book

426 English language: Rhythm
ISBN 0-521-21267-7   LC 76-7805

Library of Congress Card Number

Description of book

After discussing the nature of rhythm and "noting the effect of rhythm on poetry and prose [the author offers] . . . explanations of the relationship between speech rhythms and those of literary works, both poetry and prose. Harding, emeritus professor of psychology, University of London, . . . includes anecdotes that show how literary figures solved their problem of linking rhythms to meaning and metaphor for total effect. He includes examples of unsolved problems to illustrate lack of kinship between rhythm and a desired dramatic or emotional effect. The book grew from a series of lectures Harding prepared for Trinity College, Cambridge, England." (Choice) Bibliography. Index.

Price of book

"A wealth of information, insights, and suggestions is contained in this small volume. The . . . [author] has chosen apt and often moving examples to prove his point that modern poets and writers are not alone in having shaped their lines to the rhythms of natural speech. He affirms what we know: that a reader makes literary rhythms of his own, according to his expectations and responses. Shakespeare's poetic lines are frequently quoted to show that they were never inflexibly 'meterized,' except on purpose. . . . Highly recommended for undergraduate and graduate students in English literature."

Judgment of book

Title of periodical reviewing book; June 1977 issue of *Choice*

Choice 14:532 Je '77 220w

Review 220 words long

"My main reservation about Harding's book has to do with his insistent refusal, in his discussion of meter, to find a place for an isochronism of stresses. It is true that metrical verse fares poorly when its stresses are read, throughout, to a metronome, or even when its stresses are approximately so read. But I wish that Harding had gone beyond that observation. . . . But my reservation (along with some others) does not prevent me from assigning a high value to Harding's work, which combines a knowledge of psychology and linguistics with a detailed knowledge of the history of English literature, and discloses in its handling of examples a sustained good taste." C. L. Stevenson
J Aesthetics 35:484 summer '77 1400w

Volume and page number where review appears

Other subjects in Card Catalog under which book can be found

HARDY, BARBARA. The advantage of lyric; essays on feeling in poetry. 142p $10.95 '77 Indiana Univ. Press
821 Lyric poetry—History and criticism. English poetry—History and criticism
ISBN 0-253-30130-0   LC 76-47167

Sample entries from *Book Review Digest.*

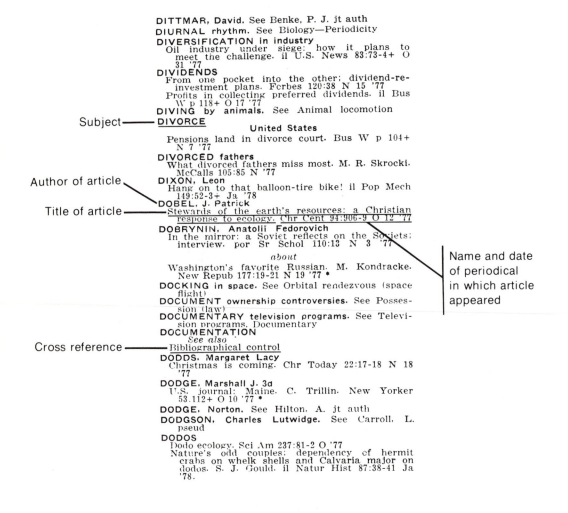

Subject ——

Author of article ——

Title of article ——

Cross reference ——

Name and date of periodical in which article appeared

DITTMAR, David. See Benke, P. J. jt auth
DIURNAL rhythm. See Biology—Periodicity
DIVERSIFICATION in industry
  Oil industry under siege; how it plans to meet the challenge. il U.S. News 83:73-4+ O 31 '77
DIVIDENDS
  From one pocket into the other; dividend-reinvestment plans. Forbes 120:38 N 15 '77
  Profits in collecting preferred dividends. il Bus W p 118+ O 17 '77
DIVING by animals. See Animal locomotion
DIVORCE
          United States
  Pensions land in divorce court. Bus W p 104+ N 7 '77
DIVORCED fathers
  What divorced fathers miss most. M. R. Skrocki. McCalls 105:85 N '77
DIXON, Leon
  Hang on to that balloon-tire bike! il Pop Mech 149:52-3+ Ja '78
DOBEL, J. Patrick
  Stewards of the earth's resources: a Christian response to ecology. Chr Cent 94:906-9 O 12 '77
DOBRYNIN, Anatolii Fedorovich
  In the mirror: a Soviet reflects on the Soviets; interview. por Sr Schol 110:13 N 3 '77

          about
  Washington's favorite Russian. M. Kondracke. New Repub 177:19-21 N 19 '77 *
DOCKING in space. See Orbital rendezvous (space flight)
DOCUMENT ownership controversies. See Possession (law)
DOCUMENTARY television programs. See Television programs, Documentary
DOCUMENTATION
    See also
  Bibliographical control
DODDS, Margaret Lacy
  Christmas is coming. Chr Today 22:17-18 N 18 '77
DODGE, Marshall J. 3d
  U.S. journal: Maine. C. Trillin. New Yorker 53.112+ O 10 '77 *
DODGE, Norton. See Hilton, A. jt auth
DODGSON, Charles Lutwidge. See Carroll, L. pseud
DODOS
  Dodo ecology. Sci Am 237:81-2 O '77
  Nature's odd couples; dependency of hermit crabs on whelk shells and Calvaria major on dodos. S. J. Gould. il Natur Hist 87:38-41 Ja '78.

Sample entries from *Readers' Guide to Periodical Literature.*

Social Sciences and Humanities Index. New York: Wilson, 1965–present. Replaced *International Index.* New York: Wilson, 1907–1965. Since 1974, published separately as *Social Science Index* and *Humanities Index.* An excellent guide to essays in scholarly journals such as the *New England Quarterly* or *Political Science Quarterly.* Includes a subject and author index.

New York Times Index. New York: The Times, 1913–present. A semimonthly and annual index to the daily issues of *The New York Times.*

Index to the Times. 1906–present. London: Times, 1907–present. A thorough bimonthly index to the *London Times.*

Newspaper Index. Wooster, Ohio: Newspaper Indexing Center, Bell and Howell, 1972–present. Indexes articles appearing in the following newspapers: *Chicago Tribune, Los Angeles Times, New Orleans Times-Picayune,* and *Washington Post.* Includes subject and author indexes.

General knowledge books: encyclopedias   The encyclopedia is the czar of general knowledge books and a good place to begin research on almost any topic. For instance, the *Encyclopaedia Britannica,* by far the best encyclopedia available, contains a useful article on "hot dogs" and "sausages," which the student consulted in doing her speech on the hot dog. Your library will no doubt have at least one or two encyclopedias on hand, and we recommend that you consult them for information on your topic.

Books about words: general and specialized dictionaries   A dictionary provides information about the meaning, derivation, spelling, syllabication, linguistic study, and usage of words. It also gives synonyms, antonyms, rhymes, slang, colloquialisms, and dialect. Specialized dictionaries exist that similarly classify and explain taboo words, slang, and colloquial expressions and phrases. Dictionaries are useful sources of definitions. Consult your librarian for information on the various dictionaries available in your library.

Books about places: atlases and gazetteers   For information about places consult any of the various atlases or gazetteers available in your library. Atlases generally contain useful maps, charts, tables, and plates that provide information about the people, culture, and economy of countries. A gazetteer is a geographical dictionary or index that gives basic information about the most important regions, cities, and natural features of the countries of the world. Researchers consult gazetteers when they want information about the legal and political status of a country, its location, and important features. Consult your librarian for information on the gazetteers available in your library.

Books about people   Numerous biographical sources are available on persons both living and dead. *The International Who's Who* provides sketches of living persons all over the world. Moreover, there are *Who's Who* volumes that list notables by both country and profession such as *Who's Who In Australia* and *Who's Who In American Politics.* For further information on the *Who's Who* volumes or on any of the various biographical dictionaries available in your library, ask the librarian.

Books about government publications   For information about government publications, ask your librarian to direct you to the various available indexes to government publications. The following are especially useful:

> U.S. Superintendent of Documents. *Monthly Catalog of United States Government Publications.* Washington, D.C.: Government Printing Office, 1895–present. A monthly catalog, arranged by departments, that provides up-to-date listings of publications from all governmental agencies. Includes subject indexes.

> U.S. Superintendent of Documents. *Checklist of United States Public Documents, 1789–1909.* 3rd ed. Washington, D.C.: Government Printing Office, 1911. Covers 120 years of government printing.

> U.S. Superintendent of Documents. *Catalog of the Public Documents of Congress and of all Departments of the Government of the United States for the Period March 4, 1893 to December 31, 1940.* 25 vols. Washington, D.C.: Government Printing Office, 1896–1945. A comprehensive summary of government materials published before 1941.

Various commercially produced guides and indexes to government publications are also available. Ask your librarian.

There are also reference books that classify information and data available on specific subjects. Depending on the complexity of your topic, a specialized reference may or may not have to be consulted. Check with your librarian about any special problems you might be having in finding material on your chosen subject.

USING ERIC: COMPUTER-ASSISTED RESEARCH

ERIC is an acronym for the Educational Resource Information Center, which is operated by the National Institute of the Department of Health, Education, and Welfare. Basically, ERIC is a nationwide system of clearinghouses that gather, coordinate, index, and catalog locally produced and unpublished materials such as project reports, speech texts, research findings, and conference reports. The sixteen ERIC clearinghouses specialize in one of the following subjects: career education; counseling and personnel services; early childhood education; educational management; handicapped and gifted children; higher education; information resources; junior colleges; languages and linguistics; reading and communication skills; rural education and small schools; science, mathematics, and environmental education; social studies and social science education; teacher education; tests, measurement, and evaluation; and urban education.

Two kinds of searches are possible under the ERIC system: a manually operated search of the ERIC references and indexes, and a computer assisted search. ERIC has indexes that catalog and classify information on one hundred thousand documents. Moreover, this information is also stored on magnetic tape for computer retrieval. In sum, if your speech topic falls under one of ERIC subject areas, it is possible that the computer in your college library may be used to help you in your research. Ask your librarian.

LOCAL SOURCES

Libraries, though especially useful, are not the only sources of information on a topic. For instance, if you were giving an informative speech on your "roots," the library would be of little use except as a source of general information on how to conduct a genealogical

search. With such a topic, the county courthouse, or some place similar where the birth and death records are kept, is more likely to yield
the kind of information you want. Likewise, depending on the topic
of your speech, the Chamber of Commerce in your area can be a
useful source for local business statistics and information.

There are numerous sources of information that students seldom
tap. Museums, traveling exhibits, and lectures can be surprisingly good
sources of information. Local police can supply up-to-date crime statistics; local pastors, doctors, and other professionals can provide
relevant testimonials. In sum, when gathering materials for your
speeches, do not overlook these sources of information available in
your community.

STEP-BY-STEP RESEARCH GUIDE

You have to give a speech, have narrowed your topic, and are
now ready to begin the research. The first step is to prepare a working bibliography.

The working bibliography

A bibliography for a speech is a list of sources on the speech
topic. These sources will range from encyclopedia entries to magazine articles to chapters or pages in books. The *working bibliography*
is a list of those sources *consulted* for information; the *final bibliography* is an alphabetical list of the sources actually *used* in drafting
the speech.

The working bibliography is assembled as the student scans the
references and card catalog for information on the subject. Some
teachers require students to enter these sources on 3×5 inch cards;
other teachers have no preference on the format used for entering the
working bibliography. As a general rule, however, bibliography cards
are better than using a scrap of paper or a page in a notebook
because they are portable, can easily be added to if a new source is
found, and can quickly be shuffled into alphabetical order, which is
how the entries have to be listed in the final bibliography.

To assemble the working bibliography, write down on a bibliography card the name of each promising source you intend to consult
for information. The card should contain information on the source,

along with a brief note on why it is likely to be useful. An example of a bibliography card prepared by a student who was giving a speech on the *Titanic* disaster is on page 92.

Generally, a student will have many more sources listed in the working bibliography than in the final bibliography. This is as it should be. Many sources will be consulted, but few will be chosen. Students must literally grope their way through the maze of sources available on the subject. Books will lure one on with a promising title and table of contents, but, once skimmed, will prove to be too technical, dated, or otherwise unuseable. The student must ignore the irrelevant and worthless source while persistently tracking down those articles, essays, speeches, and books that promise to be worthwhile and useful.

The bibliography card   Here is a summary of the form to be used on bibliography cards:

1. Record each source in ink on separate 3 × 5 inch bibliography cards.

2. Use the same form on the bibliography cards as will be used later in the final bibliography. Resist the temptation to jot down the title of the source in a secret gibberish known only to you. The final bibliography will be easy to prepare simply by copying down the information contained on the bibliography cards. The following basic information must be listed on each card:

   a. Name of author(s)
   b. Title of source
   c. Facts of publication
   d. Page(s) of information

3. In the upper right hand corner of the card, put the name of the library or place where the source was found.

4. In the upper left hand corner of the card, cite the library call number of the source so that it can be easily found even if reshelved.

Always bear in mind that the entries on the bibliography cards must contain enough information to allow an interested listener to track down and check on your source. The following, for instance, is a bibliography entry that fails to provide enough information.

Kanfer, Stefan. "The Decline and Fill of the American Hot Dog." *Time*, 2 Oct., p. 86.

The entry lists everything about the source except its year of publication—without which the source simply cannot be verified. Here is the correct listing:

Kanfer, Stefan. "The Decline and Fill of the American Hot Dog." *Time*, 2 Oct. 1972, p. 86.

Details gathered from nonliterary sources, such as personal interviews, testimonials, and the like, should be treated the same way on the bibliography cards. On page 93, for example, is a bibliography card recording details of an interview with an official of the state unemployment office.

Location of source

Library call number — G 530

College Library

Biblio-
graphic
entry

Neil, Henry

Wreck and Sinking of the Titanic

Chicago: Homewood Press, 1912

Note on why
source is
likely to
be useful

An early "memorial edition." Should be useful
as source of early reaction to the disaster.

Sample bibliography card for a book.

King, Lula (State Unemployment Counselor)

Interview conducted 2/5/78 at State Unemployment Office, 341 Kingston Street, Reno.

King was interviewed on the attitude of unemployed toward low-paying manual
labor jobs

Sample bibliography card for a nonliterary source.

Using additional sources

In your research, you should check the encyclopedia for general information on the topic you've chosen for your speech. For further sources, you should also check the bibliography at the end of an encyclopedia article. Consult standard dictionaries for definitions of abstract or technical terms. Check the card catalog in the library for books on the topic. Look up the subject in the various periodical indexes. If the topic is in the social sciences, be sure to consult the *Social Science Index*. Because articles on different subjects tend to occur in flurries, you should check both current and back volumes of the various indexes. The student doing the speech about hot dogs found nothing on her subject in the current *Reader's Guide to Periodical Literature* but discovered a handful of useful sources in the 1972 volume. For information about noteworthy persons, check the *Who's Who* volumes.

If your topic is simply too ambitious in scope, now is the time you'll find out. Sources will seem to leap at you from every corner of the library. On the other hand, if your topic is too narrow or trivial, you'll soon find yourself poring futilely over stacks of references and coming up with pitifully few sources. Be prepared to modify your topic, if necessary.

Taking notes

The information uncovered on your topic through research should be transcribed on 4 × 6 inch note cards and eventually incorporated into the body of the speech. Basically, you are hunting for supporting details that will trigger off a central idea. Once you're involved in the research, the central idea may hit you suddenly; or, it may come upon you slowly and only after you've thoroughly digested the numerous details gathered in your notes. The student, for instance, doing the speech on hot dogs, began her research with the intention of answering the question: "How nutritious are hot dogs?" When she was done, her accumulated notes reflected this consensus of opinion: Hot dogs are high in chemical additives, fat, and water; are low in protein; and often contain unacceptable quantities of bacteria. She therefore formulated the following central idea:

> The hot dog is so adulterated with chemicals, so contaminated with bacteria, so puffy with gristle, fat, water, and so lacking in protein, that it is nutritionally worthless.

Each assertion about the hot dog reflected the evidence uncovered by the student's research; now all the student had to do was to compose a speech that marshaled the appropriate supporting details behind each assertion.

The notes gathered from your research must be blended into the body of the paper to provide documentation, proof, and evidence to support the central idea. These notes are of four kinds: *summary, paraphrase, quotation,* and *personal comment.*

The summary

A summary is a condensation of significant facts from an original piece of writing. A chapter is condensed into a page, a page into a paragraph, or a paragraph into a sentence, with the condensation in each case retaining the essential facts of the original. Here is an example, showing the original and the summary as it was used in the speech:

Original: A more serious matter is mounting concern that nitrites combine, within the human body, with some amines in food to form nitrosamines. These substances have been shown to produce cancers in many species of test animals. In testimony before a House subcommittee last March, both Dr. Charles C. Edwards, commissioner of the Food and Drug Administration, and Dr. Virgil Wodicka, director of the FDA's Bureau of Foods, said that nitrites might be a factor in human cancers.

Here is the passage as it was summarized by the student and used in her speech:

Summary: Nitrites have caused cancer in laboratory animals and are a suspected cancer agent in humans.

Common sense should govern your use of the summary. Some facts and assertions need to be reported in detail; others do not and can be just as effectively summarized.

The paraphrase

To paraphrase means to say in one's own words what someone else has said. The paraphrase—unlike the summary—does not condense, but restates a passage in approximately the same number of words as the original, using the syntax and vocabulary of the paraphraser. Paraphrasing allows the student to cast the material into his or her own words, thus giving the speech an even, consistent style. Here is an example of a paraphrase.

Original: Decreasing the amount of fat in so popular a food as frankfurters might help decrease the danger of cardiovascular disease. Americans have the highest rate of atherosclerosis in the world, and such noted authorities as Dr. Jean Mayer, director of the White House Conference on Nutrition, attribute a large part of the blame to the amount of fat in the American diet.

Paraphrase: A reduction in the fat content of such a widely eaten food as the hot dog could reduce the incidence of cardiovascular disease. No people in the world suffer from atherosclerosis as much as Americans, and health experts such as Dr. Jean Mayer, who heads the White House Conference on Nutrition, put the blame largely on the quantity of fat in American foods.

The direct quotation

The quotation reproduces an author's words exactly as they were spoken or written, preserving even peculiarities of spelling, grammar, or punctuation. Use of an occasional quotation is justified where the authority of the speaker or writer is being invoked, or where the original material is so splendidly expressed as to be altogether ruined by any attempt at either summary or paraphrase.

The rules for placing quotations on note cards are:

1. Place quotation marks around the quotation.
2. Introduce the quotation or place it in its proper context.
3. Copy quotations exactly as they were written.
4. If a part of the quotation is omitted, mark the omission on the card with an ellipsis (three spaced periods).

An example of a quotation card is on page 97.
The ellipsis at the end of the quotation signifies an omission. The actual sentence read: "Children have been poisoned by the nitrite in hot dogs and bologna." "Bologna" was omitted since it is irrelevant to this speech.

The personal comment note

Personal comment notes can be used to record any ideas, conjectures, or conclusions that occur to you during the research. These notes are generally used to explicate a fuzzy statement, stress a particular point, draw a conclusion, clarify an issue, identify an inconsistency, or introduce a new idea. If the personal comment note deals with material contained on another card, staple the two cards together. An example of a personal comment note card is given on page 97.

Nitrite:
harmful effects on children

Consumer Reports
2/72, p 77

"Children have been poisoned by nitrite in hot dogs..."

Sample quotation card.

Composition of hot dogs

Personal Comment

The hot dog is a ghastly blend of chemicals, gristle, fat, water, insect parts, rodent hair, and other garbage.

Sample personal comment note card.

Notes from a nonliterary source

In recording notes gathered from a nonliterary source such as from an interview, you should observe basically the same format as would be used in any other kind of note. The card should contain information about the source along with the note. Below is an example of a note card recording information gathered from an interview with an official from the state unemployment office. The note is given as a summary.

Review of note-card format

Below is a summary of the note-card format you are expected to follow:

1. Use 4×6 inch cards for note taking. Large enough to accommodate fairly long notes, 4×6 inch cards are also unlikely to be confused with the smaller 3×5 inch bibliography cards.

Attitude of unemployed Lula King (interview)
toward menial jobs. 2/5/78

Lula King contends that the unemployed are contemptuous of low-paying menial jobs, and often choose to remain on unemployment rather than accepting such jobs. She says the state has encouraged the unemployed to accept such jobs, even temporarily, until a better position comes along.

Sample of note from a nonliterary source.

2. Write in ink so that the cards can be shuffled without blurring the notes.

3. Write down only one idea or quote on each card. Cards with only a single note can be put in any sequence simply by shuffling. If the note is so long that two cards have to be used, staple them together.

4. Identify the source of the note in the upper right hand corner of the card. Since the bibliography card already lists complete information on the source, use only the author's last name or key words from the title followed by a page number.

5. In the upper left hand corner of the card jot down a general heading for the information the card contains. These headings make it easy to organize the notes by shuffling the cards.

Bear in mind that many teachers require students to turn in the bibliography cards and note cards used in preparing a speech, and that the condition of these could affect your grade. You should therefore be as neat, accurate, and thorough as possible in making up these cards.

CHAPTER

Making an outline

"I shall never, never forget," the King said. "You will, though," the Queen said, "if you don't make a memorandum of it."

—Through the Looking Glass

THE OUTLINE AND THE CENTRAL IDEA

People have fallible memories. Most of us at one time or another have sat squirming in our seats, dying to be called on by a teacher or a moderator. Once called on, however, we mumble and falter, our splendid point forgotten, its wonderful phrasing lost. As soon as the discussion moves on, we remember what we had intended to say, and fly into a rage at our forgetfulness. Even the best speakers have had a similar experience. Memory lapses occur under the pressure of the moment; points and passages studiously researched and revised are abruptly forgotten once the speaker faces the audience. The speaker mumbles, coughs, and finally ends up improvising.

Anguish of this sort is easily preventable if you use an *outline*. You can carry the outline with you to the podium, and glance at it every so often to jog your memory. The outline simply plots out what you intend to say and how you intend to say it. In sum, the outline provides a thumbnail sketch of your entire speech.

Properly worded, the central idea can predict the principal parts of a speech, making outlining much easier. Here is an example:

Central idea: The hot dog is so saturated with chemicals, so contaminated with bacteria, so puffy with gristle, fat, and water, and so lacking in protein that it is nutritionally worthless.

In enunciating this central idea, the speaker has notified the audience of the sequence of points to be covered. Contained in the central idea is the gist of an outline. Here are the principal topics, in sequence, that will be covered in the speech:

I. The chemical content of hot dogs
II. The bacteria content of hot dogs
III. The gristle, fat, and water content of hot dogs
IV. The protein content of hot dogs

Notice how easily the topics of the speech can be extracted from the wording of the central idea. You should likewise word your central ideas in such a way as to enunciate an obvious and "outlineable" pattern to your speeches.

To predict the topics of a speech, a central idea need not be longwinded or cumbersome. Consider this central idea.

Central idea: Good writing is clear, vivid, and appropriate.

This rather straightforward central idea nevertheless contains within it the obvious gist of an outline. Clearly the speaker is obligated to speak on the following sequence of topics:

I. The clarity of good writing
II. The vividness of good writing
III. The appropriateness of good writing

The speaker simply has to accumulate definitions and examples that illustrate the clarity, vividness, and appropriateness of good writing.

The well-drafted central idea always contains, if not obvious topic divisions, at least one or two *key words* that are divisible into the major headings of an outline. Consider, for instance, these two examples:

There are numerous advantages to riding a bicycle.

The feminist movement will improve the lives of men.

The keys words are underlined. In the first example, the key word is *advantages*. The speaker is obligated, in the speech, to enumerate the advantages of bicycle riding. Here is an outline, based on a sub-division of the key word *advantages:*

    I. Advantages of economy

        A. Bicycles are inexpensive to buy.
        B. Bicycles cost little to operate.
        C. Bicycles depreciate very little.

    II. Advantages of maneuverability

        A. Bicycles are maneuverable in traffic.
        B. Bicycles are easy to park.
        C. Bicycles can be ridden almost everywhere.

    III. Advantages of exercise

        A. Bicycle riding tones the muscles.
        B. Bicycle riding strengthens the heart.
        C. Bicycle riding promotes weight loss.

In the second example, the key words are *improve, lives,* and *men.* Following is an outline based on a subdivision of these words:

    I. Improvements in social life

        A. Men will be freed from social expectations.
        B. Men will have more role choices.

    II. Improvements in business life

        A. Men will be free to choose from a wider range of careers.
        B. Men will be freed from the compulsion to succeed.

    III. Improvements in physical life

        A. Men will live longer.
        B. Men will lead fuller lives.

While other headings are possible, the principle of creating an outline remains the same: subdivision of the central idea into a series of smaller topics.

Outline format

Outlines have a visual format that can be taken in at a glance. Speakers ordinarily do not plop an outline of their speech down on a podium and then read from it. Instead, they glance casually at the outline every now and again to assure themselves that they are dealing with the major ideas of their speech in proper sequence. The permissible classroom uses of an outline will vary from teacher to teacher. Some teachers require students to construct a formal outline and submit it, along with the written text of the speech, after the speech has been delivered. Other teachers regard the outline merely as a convenience to the student and neither read nor evaluate it. Whatever the practice in your class, you should become familiar with the conventional outline format.

Main ideas are designated by Roman numerals and aligned on the page. Subideas, branching off these main ideas, are designated by capital letters and are also aligned with each other. Examples of these subideas are marked by Arabic numerals, while details supporting the examples are indicated by lowercase letters. The outline format looks like this:

> I. Main Idea
>> A. Subidea
>>> 1. Example
>>>> a. Detail
>> B. Subidea
>>> 1. Example
>>>> a. Detail
>
> II. Main Idea
>> A. Subidea
>>> 1. Example
>>>> a. Detail
>> B. Subidea
>>> 1. Example
>>>> a. Detail

In sum, major ideas are slotted to the left, and less important ideas are slotted to the right. This visual format enables a speaker to take in, at a glance, the structure of the entire speech.

Topical arrangement of headings

Various kinds of arrangements are possible in the headings of an outline. By far the commonest is the arrangement in logical order of topics. The speaker simply divides the central idea into smaller, manageable topic headings. The two outlines given earlier, on the advantages of bicycle riding and on the improvements men can expect from the feminist movement, are both topically arranged. Here is another example:

Central idea: Extremes in temperature can have dangerous effects on mountain climbers.

    I. The dangerous effects of extreme heat
       A. Heat exhaustion
       B. Heat stroke
       C. Heat cramps

    II. The dangerous effects of extreme cold
       A. Surface frostbite
       B. Body numbness
       C. Drowsiness

In making a topical outline, you must decide on the most reasonable and logical way of subdividing your central idea. Once you have chosen a principle for the subdivision, you should consistently observe it throughout the entire outline. Consider, for instance, the following outline:

Central idea: Cigarette smoking adversely affects virtually every system of the body.

    I. Adverse effects on the cardiovascular system
       A. The heart beats faster.
       B. The blood vessels constrict.

    II. Adverse effects on the digestive system
       A. The stomach secretes excess gastric acids.
       B. The appestat malfunctions.

    III. Low tar and nicotine cigarettes are better for the smoker.
       A. There is less tar and nicotine to irritate the bronchi and lungs.
       B. The level of nicotine in the blood is gradually lowered.

    IV. Adverse effects on the respiratory system
       A. The bronchial cilia are paralyzed.
       B. The bronchial sacs lose their elasticity.

Heading III is glaringly out of place. The student chose, as the most logical division of the central idea, to systematically outline the adverse effects of cigarettes on each system of the body. Heading III simply does not fit in with this scheme of outlining. It is neither predicted by the central idea nor anticipated by the audience. The inclusion of this topic therefore violates the principle on which the outline is based. This is the way the outline should look:

I. Adverse effects on the cardiovascular system
    A. The heart beats faster.
    B. The blood vessels constrict.

II. Adverse effects on the digestive system
    A. The stomach secretes excess gastric acids.
    B. The appestat malfunctions.

III. Adverse effects on the respiratory system
    A. The bronchial cilia are paralyzed.
    B. The bronchial sacs lose their elasticity.

The topical arrangement of the headings in an outline is especially suitable when the central idea consists of obvious and separate parts. Consider this central idea:

The health resources of America are inefficiently distributed and poorly organized.

The logical division that immediately suggests itself is a split of the speech into its two principal parts:

I. Inefficient distribution of health resources
II. Poor organization of health resources

Commonsense and your own innate sense of logic should dictate the most suitable principle for creating a topical outline.

Chronological arrangement of headings

Some central ideas lend themselves well to an arrangement of headings based upon progressive chronology, such as:

Throughout the years, the definition of the "second" has been constantly refined.

Implicit in this central idea is the notion of progressing chronology—exactly the principle most suitable for outlining speeches about historical subjects. Here is an outline based on a chronological arrangement of topics:

> I. In 1884, the second was defined according to the daily rotation of the earth.
>
> II. In 1960, the second was defined by the solar orbit of the earth.
>
> III. In 1967, the second was defined according to the wobble of an electron.

The principal headings in this outline are derived from a time arrangement—an arrangement especially suitable for speeches about historical subjects.

Spatial arrangement of headings

Central ideas that describe a city, a country, or a place are especially suited to an arrangement of headings based on space.

Central idea: Jamaica, called the "pearl of the Caribbean," is a variegated island.

> I. The eastern end of the island, comprising the county of Surrey, is characterized by rolling grass plains and a naturally sheltered deep-water harbor.
>
> II. The central portion of the island, comprising the county of Middlesex, is characteristically mountainous and heavily wooded.
>
> III. The western end of the island, comprising the county of Cornwall, presents a most spectacular meeting of land and ocean, boasting some of the loveliest stretches of beaches in the world.

The speech is obviously arranged to move from east to west in its description of the island. An audience would immediately grasp this arrangement and be easily able to follow it.

Problem/solution arrangement of headings

Another kind of arrangement is to outline the headings of a central idea in a problem/solution sequence. First, the speaker enumerates and catalogs the problem; then, the speaker proposes a solution and elaborates on it. Here is an example:

Central idea: The quality of the school cafeteria service could be vastly improved if it were managed by the Student Council.

Problems:

I. The school cafeteria serves poor quality food.
   A. Complaints about the cafeteria food are received every day at the Student Council office.
   B. Last year, four students were poisoned by tuna sandwiches served in the cafeteria.

II. The cafeteria operates at hours inconvenient to the student body.
   A. The cafeteria opens too late to serve students who have early classes.
   B. The cafeteria closes too early to serve students who have night classes.

Solutions:

III. The problem of poor quality food and inconvenient operating hours could be solved with Student Council management of the cafeteria.
   A. The Student Council would be able to monitor and control cafeteria food quality.
   B. The Student Council would be able to establish operating hours convenient to the students.
   C. The student body would have indirect control, through their elected representatives, over the running of the cafeteria.

This rather obvious arrangement is easy for an audience to follow. Moreover, it allows the speaker to exert considerable control over the structure and direction of the speech.

Cause/effect arrangement of headings

Finally, the headings of an outline may be arranged in a cause/effect sequence. Consider this central idea and outline:

Central idea: The diet of Americans is regarded as a contributing cause of cancer.

I. Americans consume too much red meat.
   A. Americans consume 35 percent of the world's annual meat supply.
   B. High meat consumption correlates with a high incidence of colon and breast cancers.

Cause:

II. Americans consume too little raw food fiber and roughage.
   A. Some 40 percent of the American diet consists of processed foods that, according to the Senate Select Committee on Nutrition and Human Needs, are lacking natural fiber.
   B. Lower intake of food fiber correlates with a higher incidence of intestinal cancer.

Effect:

III. Partly because of our diet, we suffer nearly the highest incidence of cancer in the world.
   A. Cancer is the number 2 killer of Americans.
   B. Cancer costs Americans nearly $2 billion per year.

The speech is divided roughly into two parts: a cataloging of cause, followed by a recital of effects. But the order could just have effectively been reversed: a recital of effects, followed by a discussion of cause, as in the following example:

Effect:

I. Partly because of our diet, we suffer nearly the highest incidence of cancer in the world.
   A. Cancer is the number 2 killer of Americans.
   B. Cancer costs Americans nearly $2 billion per year.

II. Americans consume too much red meat.
   A. Americans consume 35 percent of the world's annual meat supply.
   B. High meat consumption correlates with a high incidence of colon and breast cancer.

Cause:

III. Americans consume too little raw food fiber and roughage.
   A. Some 40 percent of the American diet consists of processed foods that, according to the Senate Select Committee on Nutrition and Human Needs, are lacking natural fiber.
   B. Lower intake of food fiber correlates with a higher incidence of intestinal cancer.

Naturally, this particular outline sequence is especially suited to speeches that set out to either enumerate causes or to catalog effects.

OUTLINE HEADINGS AND ORAL PARAGRAPHS

Students are frequently puzzled about the relationship between the individual headings in an outline and particular paragraphs in a speech. No exact formula exists, nor is one necessary. Major subdivisions in an outline are generally treated as separate paragraphs, but even this rule is not consistently observed.

Basically, you should try to give an idea the approximate emphasis it has in the outline. In other words, a minor detail should not consume entire paragraphs; a major idea should not be carelessly dismissed in one short sentence. In the excitement of speaking, you could easily become fixated on some minor point and ramble on endlessly about it, resulting in a lopsided speech and a bewildered audience. Following an outline, which more or less indicates the proportional importance of each point in the speech, will prevent you from making that mistake.

To illustrate the relationship between outline entries and paragraphs, we present the following example of an outline along with two complete paragraphs derived from it.

Central Idea: Throughout the years, the definition of the "second" has been constantly refined.

I. An early definition of the second was agreed on in 1884.
  A. The second was defined as the time it took the earth to complete 1/86,400 of its daily rotation.
  B. The earth wobbled as it rotated losing as much as 1/10 of a second annually and negating the 1884 definition.

II. The second was redefined in 1960.
  A. The second was defined as the time it took the earth to complete 1/31,556,925.9747 of its solar orbit.
  B. Atmospheric properties of the earth made the measurement of solar orbit inexact, negating the 1960 definition.

III. The second was redefined again in 1967.
   A. The second was defined as equal to 9,192,
      631,770 wobbles of a cesium electron.
   B. Time loss of only one 10 billionth of a second
      per day made the 1967 definition amazingly
      accurate.

Here are the oral paragraphs:

An early definition of the second was internationally agreed on in 1884. This definition was rather simply arrived at. It was believed that the earth made one complete rotation on its own axis every twenty-four hours. Twenty-four hours are equal to 86,400 seconds. The second was therefore defined as the time it takes the earth to complete 1/86,400 of its daily rotation.

This definition, however, was soon found to be inadequate with the discovery that the earth wobbles as it rotates. In fact, the earth resembles an unsteady, spinning top. It does not religiously complete one rotation every 86,400 seconds, as was assumed. Sometimes it is early, and sometimes late. Its rotation is affected by earthquakes, volcanic eruptions, and other large-scale natural catastrophes. On an average, it loses about 1/10 of a second per year. The definition of the second according to the rotation of the earth was therefore abandoned as inaccurate.

In sum, the entries of the outline should be transformed into reasonable oral-paragraph equivalents. For more on the construction of oral paragraphs, see Chapter 8.

Hints on preparing a useful outline

1. Observe the visual format. Properly indented outlines are much easier to read.

2. Insert as much detail as you think is necessary. Regard the outline as a memorandum to yourself. If you are the sort of speaker who is likely to become flustered and forget crucial details, you should make your outline as specific and detailed as possible.

3. Make the entries parallel. Consider, for instance, the following outline entries:

Central idea: Good writing is clear, vivid, and appropriate.

   I. The clarity of good writing

   II. Good writing is vivid

   III. The appropriateness of good writing

Obviously, such an outline will not be simple to read, especially by a speaker under stress. Contrast the above with the outline below, whose entries have parallel wording:

   I. The clarity of good writing

   II. The vividness of good writing

   III. The appropriateness of good writing

The outline with parallel entries is far easier to read at a glance.

EXERCISES

1. What obvious and logical divisions could be made of the following central ideas?

  a. The primary strokes in tennis are the ground stroke, the volley, the lob, and the overhead smash.

  b. Flying a small plane is expensive, exciting, and risky.

  c. Modern poetry is either incomprehensible or ideological.

  d. Blackjack systems are difficult to master and nearly impossible to practice under casino play conditions.

  e. The shark is a necessary and useful predator.

2. Identify the "key words" that could be subdivided in the following central ideas to create an outline.

  a. Heart disease is a killer.

  b. Cancer can be prevented.

  c. The stock market is a risky investment.

  d. Acupuncture is an effective treatment.

3. What heading sequence would you use to outline the following central ideas?

> a. The discovery of penicillin took place in many small steps over the years.
>
> b. The high crime rate in the United States could be solved by the right social programs.
>
> c. The state of California is made up of at least three distinct climatic regions.
>
> d. House plants should be well aired, well exposed, and well watered.
>
> e. Air pollution is a major cause of respiratory illness in urban areas.

4. Criticize the following brief outlines:

> a. *Central idea:* The natal horoscope of John Dillinger predicted him to be a violent, rash, and vengeful man.
>
> > I. The natal horoscope of John Dillinger predicted that he would be violent.
> >
> > II. If the Lady in Red hadn't betrayed Dillinger, he might never have been caught.
> >
> > III. John Dillinger was a rash man.
> >
> > IV. The natal horoscope of John Dillinger predicted that he would be vengeful.
>
> b. *Central idea:* The Heimlich method of saving a choking victim is effective, easy to master, and can save lives.
>
> > I. The Heimlich method of saving a choking victim is effective.
> >
> > II. People usually choke because they eat too fast and bite off more than they can swallow.
> >
> > III. The Heimlich method of saving a choking victim is easy to master.
> >
> > IV. The Heimlich method can save the life of a choking victim.

Constructing oral paragraphs

No single type of speech fits every issue or audience or speaker or occasion.

—Cicero

THE ORAL PARAGRAPH

Paragraph, a term originally meaning "something written besides," comes from medieval manuscripts where a marginal mark was used to indicate a new idea in the text. This mark eventually evolved into an indentation, and the paragraph became a square block of print on the page. When we see a new paragraph, we automatically expect either the introduction of a new idea or some other substantial shift in the discussion.

The paragraph, though a manuscript convention, is also used in speeches. Good speakers do not ramble interminably, but speak in distinctive, though invisible, blocks of thought very similar to the written paragraph. Verbal emphasis, enunciation, and pauses are used to signal these oral paragraphs.

Structure of the oral paragraph

The oral paragraph, like its written counterpart, is usually structured to proceed either from the general to the specific, or from the specific to the general. Here is an example of a paragraph with a structure proceeding from the general to the specific: a generalization is made, which is then supported by specific details.

Generalization: { But all the chemicals added to hot dogs still haven't made them pure. For example, in tests conducted on

Specific details: { hot dogs by *Consumer Reports*, only two brands tested met the maximum allowable level of contamination—10,000 bacteria per gram of meat. Forty percent of the samples analyzed—and all national brands were tested—had already begun to spoil, though they came straight off the shelves and were air shipped under refrigeration to the lab. Rodent hairs and insect parts were also found in all the samples.

In this example, the generalization is made as a declarative sentence. But it can also be made as a question, which it often is in a speech. Here is an example of an oral paragraph whose generalization is worded as a question, which is then answered by the supporting details:

Generalization worded as a question: { What does it really mean to be a hemophiliac? The first indication comes in early childhood when a small scratch

Supporting details: { may bleed for hours. By the time the hemophiliac reaches school age, he begins to suffer from internal bleeding into muscles, joints, the stomach, the kidneys. This latter type is far more serious, for external wounds can usually be stopped in minutes with topical thromboplastin or a pressure bandage. But internal bleeding can be checked only by changes in the blood by means of transfusions or plasma injections. If internal bleeding into a muscle or joint goes unchecked repeatedly, muscle contraction and bone deformity inevitably result. My crooked left arm, the built-up heel on my right shoe, and the full length brace on my left leg offer mute but undeniable testimony to that fact. Vocal evidence you hear; weak tongue muscles are likely to produce defective L and R sounds.[1]

Other paragraphs are structured to proceed from the specific to the general. Supporting details are first given, and a generalization then drawn. Here is an example:

Supporting details: { She was 882.5 feet long, 92.5 feet wide, weighed 46,328 tons at launching, and boasted a hull divided into 16 watertight compartments. She had two triple expansion reciprocating steam engines, capable of driving her along at 21 knots with virtually no vibration. She had seven grand

Generalization: { staircases, two huge leaded glass skylights, a gymnasium, hospital, swimming pool, library, post office, Turkish bath, and squash-racquets court. The *Titanic* was her name, and she was built for comfort, safety, and size, not for speed.

The generalization found in a paragraph is its topical idea and contains an assertion that the supporting details amplify, reinforce, prove, or otherwise document. The topical idea that cannot be adequately documented or supported in a single paragraph will sometimes be developed in two or three paragraphs. Here is an example taken from a speech titled, "The Unmentionable Diseases." The speaker has just described the ravages of venereal diseases, citing alarming statistics on their incidence.

Generalization worded as a question: { Why are these statistics so staggering if penicillin was such a wonderful discovery?

Supporting details that develop and answer the question: { According to Dr. Neal E. Baxter, a Bloomington physician who was the head of the V.D. research in Monroe County for several years, the first factor in this spreading problem is the mobility of the population and the loosening and decline in morals today. One sophisticated syphilitic had contacts with 171 people in 7 states and 5 foreign countries. The free-and-easy attitude toward morals is easily indicated by the Kinsey surveys, which originated at Indiana University. These reveal that a large number of American adolescents indulge in sexual experimentation—kissing, necking, petting—before they are 15 years of age. Premarital intercourse increases in frequency as adolescence progresses. By the age of 20, about 75% of the males and 40% of the females have had sexual intercourse. Promiscuity does not stop at this age level, however, as a random survey of Kinsey's pointed out that over 25% of 6,000 women interviewed had had extramarital relations before age 40.

More supporting details: { The second factor contributing to the rise of V.D. is the false public confidence in antibiotics. Since penicillin has been termed a "miracle" drug, many people, so confident in its "cure-all," have waited too long before treatment and have tried to merely get some penicillin pills from their druggist. Further research for possible cures was ended by the discovery of penicillin because Federal appropriations were cut off.

*Further answers
given in
this paragraph:*
{ The final contributing factors to the rise of V.D. are widespread ignorance and public indifference. In 1966, Dr. Daniel Rosenblatt of New York City's Health Research Council found that one-half of the students in two city colleges did not know how V.D. was contracted. In a national health test conducted by CBS television, over two-thirds of the entire population had little knowledge of venereal diseases, their symptoms, cures, or possible consequences.[2]

The topical idea developed over two or three paragraphs is, of course, more commonly found in longer speeches. In shorter speeches, the topical idea is generally developed within a single paragraph.

CHARACTERISTICS OF THE ORAL PARAGRAPH

The oral paragraph, while sharing some characteristics with its written counterpart, also has some unique features of its own. All paragraphs, whether oral or written, are characterized by unity, coherence, and emphasis. Oral paragraphs are additionally characterized by repetition and redundancy. These qualities of unity, coherence, emphasis, repetition, and redundancy are achieved in oral paragraphs by some simple grammatical structuring.

Unity

Unity refers to the strict adherence of a paragraph to the main idea contained in its topic sentence. Skilled speakers stick to the point rather than beating around the bush or punctuating their paragraphs with innumerable asides and digressions. Here, for instance, is a speaker's paragraph that lacks unity:

> The *Titanic* was considered unsinkable because she had sixteen watertight compartments with watertight doors that ran the length of her hull. The *Titanic's* builders imagined that the worst disaster that could occur would be a collision at the juncture of any two of these watertight compartments. Compared to the *Lusitania* and the *Mauretania,* the two Cunard liners the *Titanic*

> competed against, the *Titanic* was by far the more luxurious. Her sister ship the *Olympic* was almost the same size, but was slightly shorter and lighter than the *Titanic*. However, the *Olympic* outlived the *Titanic* by many years, and even saw service as a troop ship during the First World War. Since the *Titanic* could stay afloat with any two compartments flooded, or with even her first four forward compartments flooded, she was considered "unsinkable."

The unity of this paragraph is destroyed by the underlined sentences, which are entirely beside the point. It is tedious and difficult for listeners to follow speakers who wander off in such digressions. The antidote is to make one point in each oral paragraph and religiously stick to that point.

Coherence

Coherence refers to the logical integration of sentences within a paragraph. The sentences, in sum, seem held together by more than sequence of utterance out of a speaker's mouth. Obvious, logical connectives are used to integrate them. Here is an example of an incoherent paragraph:

> Although Harland & Wolff shipyards, in Belfast, Ireland, wanted the *Titanic* to be unsinkable, building her with sixteen watertight compartments was what they did to accomplish this. They knew that she could stay afloat if they were ruptured, even if two of them were flooded side by side. Whereas other ships of her day were differently built, to be safer than the *Lusitania* or the *Mauretania* was the goal of the *Titanic*. If it weren't for the freak collision with an iceberg, the sinking of the *Titanic* would never have occurred.

Under the pressure of the moment, speakers are capable of uttering this kind of gibberish. But such an oral paragraph would merely bewilder an audience, and seem nearly incomprehensible to them. Coherent paragraphs, however, can be achieved if the following suggestions are observed.

Avoid mixed constructions   Mixed constructions are sentences that begin with one grammatical pattern, then abruptly and pointlessly switch to another. The human ear is accustomed to certain regularities in the construction of sentences. For instance, when we hear this first half of a sentence:

When it snows . . . ————————➤

we anticipate this kind of completion:

◄———————— . . . children often build snowmen in the streets.

We do not, however, expect to hear something like this:

When it snows . . . the building of snowmen in the streets by children often takes place.

Obviously, this sentence, by departing unnecessarily from the anticipated pattern of completion, is rather more difficult to understand.

Consider, as another example, this opening to a sentence:

Charlene's whistling between her teeth . . . ————————➤

Ordinarily, we anticipate the sentence to end thus:

◄———————— . . . often irritates her husband.

We do not, however, expect:

Charlene's whistling between her teeth her husband is often irritated at.

Some mixed constructions are more subtle. Consider, for instance, the following sentence:

When her builders launched the *Titanic,* she was the largest ship afloat.

In the first half of the sentence "builders" is the subject; in the second half *Titanic* is the subject. Notice how much easier to understand and how more straightforward this sentence is when written this way:

When the *Titanic* was launched, she was the largest ship afloat.

The improved clarity is the result of both halves of the sentence having the same subject—the *Titanic* in the first half, and a pronoun that refers to the *Titanic* in the second half.

Your own language instincts will have to guide you in avoiding mixed constructions. If you aim at constructing straightforward oral sentences, you should have no great difficulty with mixed constructions. Often, the speaker who tries to sound highfalutin and grand is the one whose constructions are perplexingly mixed.

Use pronouns that refer to unmistakable antecedents   Pronouns should never be used unless their antecedents are unmistakably clear. Here is an example of faulty pronoun reference:

Poor: To make the *Titanic* unsinkable, her builders constructed her with sixteen watertight compartments. They knew that she could stay afloat even if they were ruptured.

Pronouns have a tendency to attach themselves to the closest noun. Though the first "they" is meant to refer to the "builders," it could be misconstrued to stand for "watertight compartments." The second "they" is nearly incomprehensible, and listeners would have a great deal of trouble understanding what it refers to.

Better: To make the *Titanic* unsinkable, her builders equipped her with sixteen watertight compartments. The builders knew that the *Titanic* could stay afloat, even if her watertight compartments were ruptured.

Beware of confusion between the expletive "it" and the pronoun "it." Here is a sentence that uses "it" as an expletive:

It is the men who must pay.

Here is a sentence that confuses the expletive "it" with the pronoun:

Poor: The object is cylindrical and blue. It can be said that it weighs more than it ought to.

The first "it" is an expletive; the second and third are pronouns.

Better: The object is cylindrical, blue, and weighs more than it ought to.

Writers and speakers will sometimes create coherence through the deliberate repetition of a pronoun that refers to a single antecedent. The repeated pronouns supply a link between the sentences. Here is an example:

Amoebae are gray bits of jelly speckled with multitudes of grains and crystals. <u>They</u> have no particular form, although when

> they're sleeping off a jag or just floating around passing the time of day, they assume a sort of star shape, like a splash of ink. Mostly they pour themselves along like a lava flow. Every once in a while they sit down on something and when they get up that something is inside them.

Express similar ideas in parallel structures   Parallel grammatical structures can be used to effectively underscore the similarity between ideas. A parallel structure simply phrases equivalent items in a similar way. Here is an example of a sentence rewritten so as not to be parallel. Notice how awkward it sounds:

> Let every nation know, whether it wishes us well or ill, that we shall pay any price, bear any burden, any hardship will be met, support any friend, oppose any foe to assure the survival and the success of liberty.

The speaker gives a catalog of sacrifices that will be met "to assure the survival . . . of liberty." Since the catalog expresses a series of equivalent ideas, all its items should be similarly phrased. The underlined entry does not begin, like the others, with a verb, and is therefore not parallel. Here is the sentence as it appeared in the speech:

> Let every nation know, whether it wishes us well or ill, that we shall pay any price, bear any burden, meet any hardship, support any friend, oppose any foe to assure the survival and the success of liberty.[3]

Here is another, more commonplace, example:

Awkward: Clearing the land, hiring the laborers, and the supervision of the architects are all part of the developer's job.

The underlined entry, unlike the others, does not begin with a participle, and the sentence is consequently not parallel.

Better: Clearing the land, hiring the laborers, and supervising the architects are all part of the developer's job.

Use transition words to help a listener follow your ideas
Transition words are often used between oral paragraphs to move the discussion smoothly from one idea to another. But they are also used within a paragraph to make it easier for listeners to follow the flow of ideas.

Although we students do bring many of our problems to campus with us, college can easily increase the intensity of some problems and create new ones. So, basically, on the college campus there are three programs that might be useful as antidotes. First is the dormitory counseling—perhaps one counselor for every 35–50 students so that these students can really become close with that counselor and develop a friendship that merits confidence. Second, a professional counseling division would be helpful where students could get vocational, academic, and personal guidance. And finally, a psychiatric division is practically essential where professional services for serious problems may be provided. These are all part of Indiana University's preventive program—and according to Dr. Frederick Coons, the university president, we have had only one suicide since 1955.[4]

The underlined words function as transitions. Numerous transition words, expressions, and phrases exist and are used by speakers to help listeners follow their arguments. Here is a partial list of some of the more commonly used transition words and phrases:

On the one hand
On the other hand
Nevertheless
In spite of
Although
Moreover
In short
In sum
Therefore
Consequently
All in all
In addition
On the whole

To sum up
First, second, third
Finally
But

Use these transition words, and others like them, to make your paragraphs more coherent.

Repeat key words in the oral paragraph   Coherence may also be achieved through the repetition of key words within a paragraph. Here is an example, taken from a speech by famed trial lawyer, Clarence Darrow:

> As to prophecies, intelligent writers gave them up long ago. In all prophecies, facts are made to suit the prophecy, or the prophecy was made after the facts, or the events have no relation to prophecies. Weird and strange and unreasonable interpretations are used to explain simple statements, that a prophecy may be claimed.[5]

Repetition of a mechanical and thudding sort can easily be carried too far. But done with moderation and commonsense, the repetition of key words within a paragraph can aid in coherence.

Emphasis

Emphasis is achieved by the expression of more important ideas in main or independent clauses, and of less important ideas in subordinate or dependent clauses. In other words, an utterance that is properly emphatic will rank ideas through grammatical structure. Here is a simple example of an unemphatic utterance made emphatic through subordination:

Unemphatic: The doctors fought to save her life. She herself was brave and spirited to the end. The tumor eventually killed her.

Emphatic: Although the doctors fought to save her life and she herself was brave and spirited to the end, the tumor eventually killed her.

The second construction assigns a main clause to the most important idea, "the tumor eventually killed her," and a subordinate clause to the less important ideas, "Although . . . the end." By this grammatical structuring, the relative importance of each idea is thus made clear.

Skilled speakers habitually word their speeches in such a way as to make their principal ideas more emphatic. Consider, for instance, the following two examples, the first, unemphatic and the second, emphatic:

> The state of Mississippi swelters with the heat of injustice. The state of Mississippi swelters with the heat of oppression. I have a dream. One day even the state of Mississippi will be transformed into an oasis of freedom and justice.

> I have a dream that one day, even the state of Mississippi, a state sweltering with the heat of injustice, sweltering with the heat of oppression, will be transformed into an oasis of freedom and justice.[6]

Chapter 9 on language contains a full discussion of emphasis. For now, you should be aware that emphatic wording is a characteristic of well-constructed paragraphs.

Repetition

Because of the invisibility of the spoken word, oral paragraphs are inevitably more repetitious than written paragraphs. Speakers have to speak carefully and repetitiously or they run the risk of being misunderstood. Propositions are stated and restated; complex notions are elaborated on; crucial statements are repeated. Numerous examples of repetition in oral paragraphs can be found:

> The fourth observation I wanted to make is that some patients may have a mental illness and then get well, and then may even get "weller"! I mean they get better than they ever were. They get even better than they were before.[7]

> We can never be satisfied as long as our bodies, heavy with the fatigue of travel, cannot gain lodging in the motels of the highways and the hotels of the cities. We cannot be satisfied as long as the Negro's basic mobility is from a smaller ghetto to a larger one.
>
> We can never be satisfied as long as our children are stripped of their selfhood and robbed of their dignity by signs stating "for whites only." We cannot be satisfied as long as a Negro in Mississippi cannot vote and a Negro in New York believes he has nothing for which to vote. No, we are not satisfied, and we will not be satisfied until justice rolls down like waters and righteousness like a mighty stream.[8]

Repetition is primarily used in the oral paragraphs of longer speeches. In constructing your own oral paragraphs, use repetition, with moderation, to explain any complex ideas or to emphasize any crucial issue.

Redundancy

Redundancy—sometimes called "wordiness"—occurs whenever a speaker, either for emphasis or clarity, deliberately overstates a condition, proposition, or idea. In writing, redundancy is a cardinal sin most often committed by the inexperienced. But in oral paragraphs, again because of the invisibility of the spoken word, speakers are often usefully and necessarily redundant. Here is an example:

> Others will debate the controversial issues, national and international, which divide men's minds. But serene, calm, aloof, you stand as the nation's war guardians, as its lifeguard from the raging tides of international conflict, as its gladiator in the arena of battle. For a century-and-a-half you have defended, guarded, and protected its hallowed traditions of liberty and freedom, of right and justice.[9]

The underlined expressions and words can surely be considered unnecessary in a strict rhetorical sense. Nevertheless, the redundancy of the paragraph dramatically adds to its impact, if not to its literal meaning.

Redundancy is a subtle device that should be used with caution. Paragraphs bloated with synonyms are often tedious to listen to and difficult to understand. Nevertheless, bearing in mind that your audience can only hear your words, you should phrase your ideas as redundantly as necessary to make them clear.

SPECIAL KINDS OF ORAL PARAGRAPHS

Our discussion has so far centered on the informational oral paragraph, that is, the paragraph structured to provide a listener with material that clarifies, amplifies, and documents a generalization. Various other kinds of oral paragraphs perform other functions and are structured differently. Among these are the following.

The introductory oral paragraph

The structure and content of the introductory oral paragraph varies with the purpose and length of the speech. In short speeches, the primary function of the introductory paragraph is to state the central idea.

Central idea: { Many people have made their expressed purpose in life that of either proving or disproving the existence of God by the use of scientific data. Let me point out immediately that what I'm going to do today is neither of these. What I'm going to try to show is that man's scientific agruments, by which I mean arguments drawn from any natural phenomenon, cannot possibly prove or disprove the existence of God.[10]

Note that the paragraph is not structured to have a generalization that is then documented by supporting details. Its function is not to document a generalization but to introduce a central idea.

In longer speeches, the introductory oral paragraph is used to establish friendly contact between the audience and speaker. The speaker will either say how happy he or she is to be there or will find some means of establishing rapport with the audience.

It is a pleasure to be in Denver once more, to visit again this university where I taught one happy summer, and to have the opportunity to renew so many long standing and precious friendships. Actually, I tend, in retrospect, to associate this institution with one of the major changes in the direction of my life. It was here that I enjoyed my last full-time teaching—though I did not know it at the time—because immediately after my return from that pleasant summer here I was invited to become the Provost of Columbia, a decision that, once made, brought my teaching days to a close. Now that I am here again, who knows but that when I get back to New York there might be a strong campus opinion developed in my absence in favor of my return to teaching. If this should be the case, then I think I ought to come back here and start where I left off in 1949.[11]

This paragraph obviously has little to do with the proposed topic of the speech, except to establish a relationship between the speaker and the audience. Various other openings can be used to gain the attention and goodwill of an audience, and these are widely practiced in longer speeches. The point of this discussion, however, is that introductory paragraphs perform a special function and are consequently structured differently from informational paragraphs.

The transitional oral paragraph

Transitional oral paragraphs, as the name implies, are used to move the speech from one major point to another. Generally, they are short paragraphs containing only a sentence or two. Here is a typical example:

This, of course, is not quite like the notion of some physical diseases. One can have many degrees of arthritis. But one either *has* malaria or does not have it. The same is true with many other diseases. But in the case of mental illness, it seems that any of us can—indeed, all of us *do*—have some degree of it, at some time.

That is my first observation. Now for a second observation.

The general notion has long prevailed that, once mental illness has appeared, the victim is doomed. The illness progresses, the disability increases, the specter of dementia looms inevitably ahead. . . .[12]

The second paragraph is obviously there to ease the transition from one major point to another. Usually, after the transitional paragraph, the speaker will pause before proceeding with added emphasis to the opening sentence of the next oral paragraph.

The concluding oral paragraph

Concluding oral paragraphs often contain sweeping summaries of notions that the body of the speech has sought to prove. Here are two examples:

> There must be no state church and no required religion. But good religion supports legitimate government, and good government is on the side of ethical religion.[13]

> When we understand that these two major stumbling blocks to the educational progress of the underprivileged children can be eliminated—that they can be encouraged to communicate and that apathy and antagonism can be conquered—we realize that we need not write these children off as a lost cause. We need not lose these valuable human resources. We can help the "unteachables" to discover the magic of learning and achieving. We can help them to understand Schulz's definition: "Happiness is finding out you're not so dumb after all."[14]

If the speech is an exhortation, its final paragraph will often appeal to the audience for help. Here, for instance, is the final paragraph from a speech on hemophilia delivered by a hemophiliac:

> I cannot change that part of my life which is past. I cannot change my hemophilia. Therefore I must ask you to help those hemophiliacs that need help. For I remember too well my older brother Herbert, so shattered in adolescence by hemophilia that his tombstone reads like a blessing: "May 10, 1927–April 26, 1950, Thy Will Be Done." And I ask you to help hemophiliacs because one day my grandson may need your blood. . . .[15]

The content of the final paragraph will vary with the purpose and the content of the speech. Moreover, this paragraph—as the last in the speech—will often consist of an appeal to the audience, a summary of the points covered in the speech, or a statement of what good results can be expected if the speaker's recommendations are followed.

TURNING NOTES INTO AN ORAL PARAGRAPH

You have done research on your subject, compiled notes, and tentatively sketched an outline of the speech. The next step is to transform your notes into individual oral paragraphs. Exactly how much writing you will have to do depends on your teacher. Some teachers require students to actually compose the speech on paper and then deliver it before the class. Other teachers expect their students to speak extemporaneously from their notes and outline. A third group of teachers require their students to deliver the speech from their notes and outline, and then to submit the speech in written form. Your teacher will make it clear exactly what you are required to do.

If you have done the research properly, the process of turning your notes into paragraphs can be rather automatic, for the quality of a paragraph invariably depends on the quality of its details. Packed with interesting details, the paragraph will seem fresh and lively; lacking such details the paragraph will sound wishy-washy and dull. Nor can clever wording or cute images compensate for the emptiness of a paragraph. In sum, if you wish to construct good oral paragraphs, you must first be in possession of the facts. Here are some suggestions for constructing your paragraphs.

Develop a single idea in each paragraph   Speakers have to be especially careful to restrict the coverage of their paragraphs to a single, comprehensible idea, or they run the risk of baffling their audiences. We suggest that you word the generalizations of your paragraphs to express a single idea that can be adequately documented with supporting details. Here are two examples, one wrong, the other right:

> *Poor:*   There are five venereal diseases, all of which can cause death, but penicillin can cure them if it is used early enough.

The generalization commits the speaker to discuss two separate ideas: kinds of venereal disease and penicillin as a cure. It is impossible to adequately support both topics in a single paragraph without thoroughly confusing the audience. Poorly worded generalizations are the commonest flaws of student paragraphs. Moreover, it is a flaw easily corrected by diligence and effort.

> *Better:* There are five venereal diseases, all of which can cause death. Three of these have been eliminated by modern medicine, while the other two, syphilis and gonorrhea, are on the rise once more all over the world. Both of these diseases are mainly contracted through sexual relations. These germs spread to all parts of the body, and, therefore, anything the infected person uses is possibly an immediate carrier. These germs can spread to another human by an open cut if it comes in close contact with the germs of the infected person.[16]

Word generalizations to interpret supporting details   The purpose of the generalization in a paragraph is not only to further the discussion, but also to interpret the supporting details. Uninterpreted details are meaningless. It is not enough to simply pack a paragraph with facts; the audience must also be told what the facts mean. Here are two examples:

> *Poor:* Last year I was disturbed to read an article in the *Saturday Evening Post* entitled, "Youth—The Cool Generation." It was written by Dr. Gallup and Evan Hill and was based on 3,000 interviews with young people up to the age of 22. The article stated that the typical youth will settle for low success rather than risk high failure; that he has little spirit of adventure; that he wants little because he has so much, and is unwilling to risk what he has.

One might ask, so what? The generalization of a paragraph should answer exactly such a question.

> *Better:* The idea of security seems to have grown so rapidly in recent years that the spirit of risk-taking—historically

the dominant mark of youth—has become somewhat dulled. Last year I was disturbed to read an article in the *Saturday Evening Post* entitled, "Youth—The Cool Generation." It was written by Dr. Gallup and Evan Hill and was based on 3,000 interviews with young people up to the age of 22. The article stated that the typical youth will settle for low success rather than risk high failure; that he has little spirit of adventure; that he wants little because he has so much, and is unwilling to risk what he has.[17]

The uninterpreted detail is not worth giving. Do not, therefore, simply stockpile details in your paragraphs. Use details to support your generalizations; use generalizations to interpret your details.

Finally, we do not wish to leave you with the impression that paragraphs are spoken or written according to some rigid, exact, universal pattern. No product of language can be neatly compressed into any sort of inviolable mold. What we have been discussing are paragraphs that conform to the norm, to the ordinarily used and often followed model. Nevertheless, considerable variation is to be found among paragraphs, as can be reasonably expected in the creative use of language.

EXERCISES

1. Identify the generalizations in the following paragraphs:

    a. In testimony before the same Senate committee, Newark Airport officials reported that as early as 1946 the number of hours in which visibility was cut to six miles or less by smoke alone, or in combination with other factors, totaled 4,359 hours that year —nearly 50% of the total hours during the year. On some occasions air pollutants alone were even sufficient to ground planes at Idlewild airport. In reviewing accident cases for 1962, the Civil Aeronautics Board listed six cases in which obstruction of view due to air pollution was the primary cause. On this basis, since 1960, 50 aeronautical accidents may well have been due to atmospheric pollution. Thus, air pollution fulfills another role on the criminal roster—that of crippler, maimer, and indiscriminate killer in automobile and air accidents.
    —Charles Schalliol, "The Strangler," Indiana Oratorical Association Contest, Bloomington, Indiana, 1967.

b. Although each case is different, what are some of the general motives for suicide? College psychiatrists, deans, and heads of counseling list several. One would be our search for identity—this has to do with breaking away from home and becoming an adult. Every parent knows that some day his child is going to become an adult. Some parents help their children to accept St. Paul's admonition to "put away childish things." Others don't. As a result, students frequently find themselves being pushed out of their homes, where they have been children, into a college situation where they must be adults.

> —Patricia Ann Hayes, "Madame Butterfly and the Collegian," Indiana Oratorical Association Contest, Bloomington, Indiana, 1967.

c. There has been a deterioration in the literary style of speeches. Politicians, lawyers, and ministers, the ranks from which most of our speakers are drawn, live in a busy and hurried age; they have less and less time for reading, reflection, and the maturing of their own literary styles; they do not read the masters and the classics as they once did. They are readers of newspapers and periodicals in an age when newspapers and periodicals are less literary and more journalistic. Practitioners of the art of public speaking today are apt to piece together a speech from newspaper clippings and current editorials. Or worse still, the busy public man, engrossed with a thousand and one duties and increasingly dependent upon experts in technical fields for the intellectual materials covering his job, calls upon numerous ghost writers to prepare his speeches. Paragraphs from many sources are then assembled and fitted into the speech.

> —William G. Carleton, "Effective Speech in a Democracy," Southern Speech Association, April 1951.

2. The following paragraphs have been deliberately tampered with to destroy their unity. Identify and excise the extraneous sentences.

a. Primitive and even civilized people have grown so accustomed to believing in miracles that they often attribute the simplest manifestations of nature to agencies of which they know nothing. They do this when the belief is utterly inconsistent with knowledge and logic. Aristotle, as everyone here knows, was the supreme logician of all times. The deductive syllogism, which Francis Bacon heaped such contumely upon, and unfairly, I might add, nevertheless served mankind as the staple process for reasoning for over a thousand years. In spite of Aristotle and Bacon and the army of logicians before and after, people still remain superstitious. They believe in old miracles and new ones. Preachers pray for rain, knowing fully well that no such prayer was ever answered. When a politician is sick, they pray for God to cure him, and the politician invariably dies. The modern clergyman who prays for rain and for the health of the politician is no more intelligent in this matter than the primitive man who saw a separate miracle in the rising and setting of the sun, in the birth of an individual, in the growth of a plant, in the stroke of lightning, in the flood, in every manifestation of nature and life.

b. Darwin's principle of natural selection, based as it is on constant pressure of competition or struggle, has been invoked to justify various policies in human affairs. For instance, it was used, especially by politicians in late Victorian England, to justify the principles of *laissez-faire* and free competition in business and economic affairs. If Germany had not so over-extended herself simultaneously on two fronts, there is no telling how the Second World War might have ended. The greatest blunder the Germans made was to launch their attack on Russia so late. And it was used, especially by German writers and politicians from the late nineteenth century onwards, to justify militarism. War, so ran this particular version of the argument, is the form which is taken by natural selection and the struggle for existence in the affairs of the nations. Without war, the heroic virtues degenerate; without war, no nation can possibly become great or successful.

3. Identify the most obvious technique used to maintain coherence in the following paragraphs.

a. You might ask—but what can I do? What do you expect of me? The answer lies in the title of this oration: mingled blood. For all that boy needs is blood, blood, and more blood. Blood for transfusions, blood for fresh-frozen plasma, blood for serum fractions. Not Red Cross Bank Blood, for stored blood loses its clot-producing factors. But fresh blood directly from you to him in a matter of hours. Your blood, dark and thick, rich with all the complex protein fractions that make for coagulation—mingled with the thin, weak, and deficient liquid that flows in his veins. Blood directly from you to the medical researcher for transformation into fresh-frozen plasma or antihemophilic globulin. During those years, his very life is flowing in your veins. No synthetic substitute has been found—only fresh blood and its derivatives.

b. The motor car is, more than any other object, the expression of the nation's character and the nation's dream. In the free billowing fender, in the blinding chromium grills, in the ever-widening front seat, we see the flowering of the America that we know. It is of some interest to scholars and historians that the same autumn that saw the abandonment of the window crank and the adoption of the push button (removing the motorist's last necessity for physical exertion) saw also the registration of sixteen million young men of fighting age and symphonic styling. It is of deep interest to me that in the same week Japan joined the Axis, De Soto moved its clutch pedal two inches to the left—and that the announcements caused equal flurries among the people.

c. Of course, humor is often more than a laughing matter. In its more potent guises, it has a Trojan-horse nature: No one goes on guard against a gag; we let it in because it looks like a little wooden toy. Once inside, however, it can turn a city to reform, to rebellion, to resistance. Some believe, for instance, that, next to the heroic British RAF, British humor did the most to fend off German takeover in World War II. One sample will suffice: that famous story of the woman who was finally extracted from the rubble of her house during the London blitz. Asked, "Where is your husband?" she brushed brick dust off her head and arms and answered, "Fighting in Libya, the bloody coward!"

4. Rewrite the following sentences to make them parallel.

   a. She needs its warm sweetness before the night is out to escape her fears, her guilt, and the remorse she feels.

   b. They sold their house, their furniture, and the boat they owned.

   c. Patience, diligence, and paying painstaking attention to detail— these are the requirements.

   d. As the shoreline lives, decays, and is devoured by itself, it gives birth to numerous, lovely creatures.

   e. It is harder to hate people as a whole than hating one's neighbor.

NOTES

[1]Ralph Zimmerman, "Mingled Blood," Interstate Oratorical Contest, 1955.

[2]Mary Katherine Wayman, "The Unmentionable Diseases," Indiana University, Bloomington, Indiana, 1967.

[3]John F. Kennedy, Inaugural Address, Washington, D.C., 20 January 1960.

[4]Patricia Ann Hayes, "Madame Butterfly and the Collegian," Indiana Oratorical Association Contest, Bloomington, Indiana, 1967.

[5]Clarence Darrow, "Why I Am an Agnostic," symposium on religion, Columbus, Ohio, 1929.

[6]Martin Luther King, Jr., "I Have a Dream," Washington, D.C., August 1963.

[7]Karl Menninger, "Healthier Than Healthy," New York City, 5 April 1958.

[8] Martin Luther King, Jr., "I Have a Dream."

[9] Douglas MacArthur, "Farewell to the Cadets," West Point, New York, 12 April 1962.

[10] Leon R. Zeller, "What Can We Prove About God?" Pennsylvania State University, University Park, Pennsylvania, 1965.

[11] Grayson Kirk, "Responsibilities of the Educated Man," University of Denver, Denver, Colorado, 1964.

[12] Karl Menninger, "Healthier Than Healthy."

[13] Howard C. Wilkinson, "How Separate Should Government and God Be?" Charlotte Executive Club, Charlotte, North Carolina, 1963.

[14] Carolyn Kay Geiman, "Are They Really Unteachable?" University of Kansas, Lawrence, Kansas, 1964.

[15] Ralph Zimmerman, "Mingled Blood."

[16] Mary Katherine Wayman, "The Unmentionable Diseases."

[17] Gerald Lynch, "The Pursuit of Security," Commencement Speech, University of Dayton, Dayton, Ohio, 1963.

9

Wording the speech

Except as ye utter by the tongue words easy to understand, how shall it be known what is spoken? For ye shall speak into the air.

—St. Paul

CHARACTERISTICS OF WORDS

When the gloomy Hamlet, Prince of Denmark, was asked what he was reading, he replied rather airily, "Words, words, words," as if to contemptuously dismiss the entire lexicon. Indeed, words that are misused and twisted can cause a terrific muddle. But used sparingly and with precision, words can communicate a great deal.

The kinds of words that do well on paper are not likely to be as effective in utterance. Nor, for that matter, are words that sound well especially effective when written on the page. Speaking and writing, as we have been emphasizing, are different forms of communication. Words chosen to be spoken rather than to be written need to be shorter, more concrete, and more familiar. The abstract and unfamiliar word fares better on the page than in the mouth. As readers, we can check a dictionary or reread a passage; as listeners, we simply stop listening.

Every speech is composed of three linguistic parts: words, sentences, and oral paragraphs, and each of these, in turn, is affected by the nature and demands of orality. We have already talked about oral paragraphs. In this chapter, we will talk about words and sentences that might be effectively used in a speech.

Representational words

Words stand for things, objects, and ideas. When children first learn to talk, they are carefully taught the names of things by their parents. "Dog" says the parent, pointing to the family poodle. "Dog?" queries the child, looking a little mystified. Eventually, through this kind of repetition, the child learns that the word *dog* stands for the familiar four-legged creature.

Without reflection, the advantage of this sort of naming is little appreciated. Words allow us to miniaturize the objects and items in our universe and carry them conveniently around in our heads. We can sit at a cafe and talk about bulldozers, parrots, and pyramids without either a bulldozer, parrot, or pyramid being anywhere near in sight. Most people carry around a great number of words in their heads. Journalists regularly use a vocabulary of about twenty-thousand words; doctors, lawyers, and clerics use about ten thousand words; skilled workers use a vocabulary of nearly five thousand words. Sciences and the learned professions have their own specialized vocabularies, which the person on the street rarely ever hears. Medicine, for instance, has names for some 433 muscles, 193 veins, 707 arteries, 500 pigments, 295 poisons, 109 tumors, 700 tests, 200 diseases, and some 3,000 bacteria. Through words the wisdom of one age is stored and passed on to another.

Abstract and concrete words

Semanticists classify words into two large groups: abstract words and concrete words. Abstract words represent conditions, ideas, notions, and concepts. Words such as *love, hate, liberty* represent states of being and are therefore classified as abstract. Concrete words, on the other hand, stand for tangible, visible objects. The word *apple* is concrete because it represents an object that can be seen and pointed to. Of these two kinds of words, abstract words are obviously the more likely to be misunderstood.

The extent of the misunderstanding possible is evident from the diagram, known as a *semantic triangle,* shown on the opposite page. According to the semantic triangle, the meaning of a word is divisible into two parts: its *reference* and its *referent*. The referent of a word is the thing, object, or idea that the word represents. For instance, the referent of the word *apple* is obviously the fruit we know by that

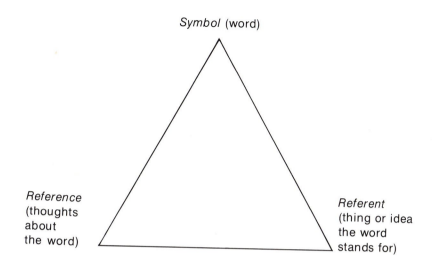

name. On the other hand, the referent of the word *love* is the heart-palpitating, palm-sweating condition that men and women all over the world occasionally claim to suffer. Dictionaries catalog the common referents of words and can be consulted to settle any disagreements over the literal meaning of a word.

Disagreements over references, however, cannot be settled by a dictionary. For references are the thoughts and emotions that different words evoke from different people. Here is a semantic triangle showing how the word *marriage* might appear to a recently and bitterly divorced woman.

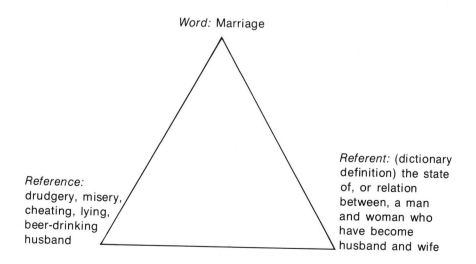

On the other hand, here is how the word *marriage* might appear to a happily married man.

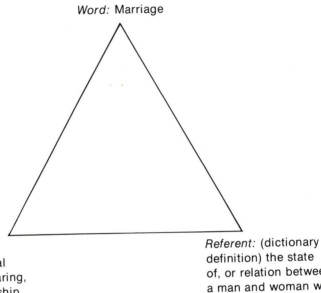

Word: Marriage

Reference:
bliss, connubial
happiness, sharing,
loving partnership

Referent: (dictionary
definition) the state
of, or relation between,
a man and woman who
have become husband
and wife

Negative references might also exist for a concrete word. For instance, a man who has once nearly choked to death on an apple is not likely to respond to the word *apple* as benignly as the woman who has eaten hundreds of apples with no ill effects. Nor, for that matter, is the survivor of a shark attack likely to regard the word *shark* in the same way as the person who has only seen a shark on a movie screen. All of us have accumulated personal experiences that cause us to react uniquely to words.

The semantic triangle should teach you two lessons about word usage. The first lesson is that abstract words crucial to the ideas of a speech should be carefully defined. The more abstract the word, the fuzzier the referent, and the greater the chance of misunderstanding.

For instance, if you were giving a speech on "The Function of Love in Family Life," you had better begin by making it clear what you mean by *love*—a word so abstract that it is not even uniformly defined in dictionaries. A concrete word such as *hot dog*, on the other hand, need not be defined since it is not likely to be misunderstood.

The second lesson taught by the semantic triangle is that the dictionary definition of a word is not always an accurate gauge of how an audience is likely to react to it. If individuals can have different references for the same words, so can groups. *Socialized medicine,* used before separate audiences of the chronically ill and of prosperous physicians, will have vastly different references. The word *abortion* may provoke one reaction from an audience of feminists and quite another from an audience of Catholic clergy. In sum, while you will never be able to foretell exactly how an audience might react to your words, you should nevertheless consider the make-up of the audience in wording the speech and try to choose words that will neither provoke, alienate, nor offend.

Abstractness of words   Words vary in abstractness. Consider, for instance, if you wanted to talk about the work of the poet Shelley. Below are a number of words, arranged from the most abstract to the most concrete, which could be used to describe Shelley's work. "Shelley's writing" is more abstract than "Shelley's poetry," "Shelley's poetry" is more abstract than "Shelley's sonnets," and "Shelley's 'Ozymandias' " is the most specific of all, since it is the name of a particular sonnet by Shelley.

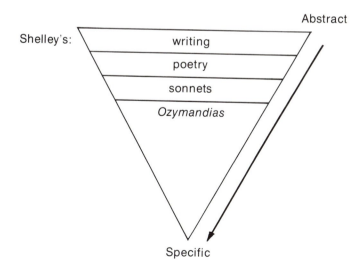

Depending on the words a speaker uses, a topic may be discussed in varying degrees of abstractness. The vocabulary of student speakers, as a matter of fact, tends to be abstract rather than specific. Consider, for instance, this oral paragraph from a student speech:

> Cigarette smoke contains many harmful substances including known cancer agents. These substances affect many parts of the respiratory system. Elements in cigarette smoke affect the cilia—the small waving hairs lining the bronchial tubes—which are responsible for clearing the respiratory system of foreign matter. Moreover, things found in cigarette smoke are deposited in many parts of the body, where they accumulate.

The underlined words and phrases are abstract and vague enough to make the entire paragraph sound fuzzy. Here is a rewrite that replaces the underlined expressions with more concrete words:

> Cigarette smoke contains gases, uncondensed vapors, and liquid particulates, including the chemical benzo(a)pyrene, the deadliest known cancer agent. Gases, such as carbon monoxide, formaldehyde, and hydrogen cyanide, found in cigarette smoke, paralyze the cilia—the small waving hairs lining the bronchial tubes—which are responsible for clearing the respiratory system of bacteria and particulates. Moreover, particles found in cigarette smoke are deposited in the larynx, carina, major bronchi, smaller bronchi, bronchioles, and pulmonary tissue, where they accumulate.

Below are two columns, one listing the abstract word or phrase used in the first version of the oral paragraph, the other listing the more concrete replacement that was used in the second version.

Abstract	*Concrete*
many harmful substances	gases, uncondensed vapors, and liquid particulates
known cancer agents	the chemical benzo(a)pyrene, the deadliest known cancer agent

Abstract	*Concrete*
These substances	Gases, such as carbon monoxide, formaldehyde, and hydrogen cyanide
affect	paralyze
foreign matter	bacteria and particulates
things	particles
many parts of the body	larynx, carina, major bronchi, smaller bronchi, bronchioles, and pulmonary tissue.

The more concrete you are, the more authoritative and expert your speech will sound. Nothings hints of amateurishness more quickly than the use of vague, abstract references and terms.

Meaning of Words   English has an immense vocabulary. It contains numerous abstract words that have an impressive and dignified ring but are vague to the point of meaninglessness. The repeated use of these words create gobbledygook—talk or writing that sounds pompous, wordy, and silly. To illustrate how the overuse of abstract words creates gobbledygook, we reproduce below the "Bafflegab Thesaurus," which originated from a Royal Canadian Air Force listing of fuzzy words. Any word from column A, matched with any word from columns B and C, will produce abstract, yet lofty-sounding, nonsense.

	A	B	C
1.	integrated	management	options
2.	total	organizational	flexibility
3.	systematized	monitored	capability
4.	parallel	reciprocal	mobility
5.	functional	digital	programming
6.	responsive	logistical	concept
7.	optional	transitional	time-phase
8.	synchronized	incremental	projection
9.	compatible	third-generation	hardware
10.	balanced	policy	contingency

What we have been trying to teach you is simply this: While you want to include compatible reciprocal concepts in your speech; while you want to give the instructor the impression that you have total management capability over your subject; and while you understandably desire to present your audience with synchronized third-generation options; nevertheless, if you wish to make sense, you should avoid the big, abstract word and choose, instead, the familiar and the concrete word.

Finally, do not be deluded into thinking that the bigger and more abstract the words, the more moving and impressive a speech is likely to sound. Wondrously grave statements have been made with short, simple words. Here is a striking example of the power of short, familiar words:

> I am tired of fighting. Our chiefs are killed. Looking Glass is dead. Toohulsote is dead. The old men are all dead. It is the young who say no and yes. He who led the young men is dead. It is cold and we have no blankets. The little children are freezing to death. My people, some of them, have run away to the hills and have no blankets, no food. No one knows where they are—perhaps they are freezing to death. I want to have time to look for my children and see how many of them I can find. Maybe I shall find them among the dead. Hear me, my chiefs, I am tired. My heart is sad and sick. From where the sun now stands I will fight no more forever.[1]

Words have sounds

A rather obvious observation, no doubt, but one often overlooked by students used to setting their words soundlessly down on paper. In a speech, however, the sounds of words should be considered an important factor in word choice.

Speakers should use words somewhat like poets do. Poets—whose language style is primarily oral—have consistently chosen words for their sounds as well as for their meanings. For instance, it is a commonsense observation that long, multisyllable words, since they take longer to pronounce, tend to slow down a line. Consequently, a poet wishing to create a mood of languorous slowness will often achieve this effect by deliberately packing long words in a sentence. Consider, for instance, these two lines by Alfred, Lord Tennyson:

> The moan of doves in immemorial elms,
> And murmuring of innumerable bees.

Words can also be chosen to deliberately quicken the tempo of a line, as in this example from a poem by John Milton:

> Swift as the sparkle of a glancing star.

The considerations involved in choosing words for a speech are different from those involved in choosing words for a poem. The poet wishes to reinforce meaning with sound; the speaker wishes to be *instantly intelligible.* Words chosen for a speech should be concrete, familiar, and easily pronounced, otherwise a speaker is likely to find himself saying a proverbial "mouthful." Short, simple words, while being easier to pronounce, are also easier for an audience to hear and instantly understand. Here is a passage written to be read rather than spoken. Notice how ponderous and wooden its words sound when read aloud:

> Objective consideration of contemporary phenomena compels the conclusion that success or failure in competitive activities exhibits no tendency to be commensurate with innate capacity, but that a considerable element of the unpredictable must invariably be taken into account.

Here is the same general idea, worded in an oral style, and taken from the most oral of books, the Bible:

> I returned and saw under the sun, that the race is not to the swift, nor the battle to the strong, neither yet bread to the wise, nor yet riches to men of understanding, nor yet favor to men of skill; but time and chance happeneth to them all.

Aside from mouthing unintelligible nonsense, the speaker who uses long, difficult to pronounce words in a speech also runs the risk of sounding harsh and cacophonous. Cacophony occurs when words are uttered in a combination that makes an unpleasant and grating sound. Writers, though their words will be internally read by different readers, worry less about cacophony since it is more difficult to detect on the page than in the utterance. Here is an example of a cacophonous sentence:

> Blatant mistakes of gargantuan dimensions characterize this report.

Read aloud, the sentence seems made up of fire-cracker syllables that pop and explode in the speaker's mouth. As you practice your speech, cacophonous sentences such as this should become obvious.

Cacophony is not the only sound effect you need to be wary of in wording your speech. You should also be alert to peculiar word combinations that might produce an internal rhyme. Even the loftiest idea sounds silly when stated in a rhyming sentence. The following sentence, from a BBC broadcast, is mistakenly worded to contain internal rhymes:

> The enemy is <u>reported</u> to have seized this <u>important</u> <u>port</u>, and reinforcements are hurrying up in sup<u>port</u>.

Unintentional alliteration—where initial consonants of words sound alike—can also make a sentence sound ludicrous:

> Perhaps his puny profits pose no persistently serious problem.

Alliteration and rhymes, though suitable sound effects for a poem, do not belong in a speech, unless used intentionally for a burlesque effect.

Words have denotations and connotations

The denotation of a word is the object, idea, or event with which the word can be exactly matched. *Pig,* for instance, denotes the specific animal known by that name. *Love* denotes a specific emotional state. *Turkey* denotes a particular bird, and *tiger* denotes a particular kind of predatory cat. Denotative meaning is therefore nothing more nor less than the exact referent of a word.

But words mean more than they exactly denote. Words reflect the characteristics of their referents as secondary meanings. The turkey, for instance, is an ungainly, stupid bird, given to hideous gobbling and pointless strutting. The turkey is so stupid that it is rather an easy prey. When you call someone a "turkey" you don't mean to say that he gobbles, struts, and is ungainly; you mean to say that he is stupid and easily duped. This kind of implied meaning is known as connotation.

Skillful writers and speakers use words to denote and connote. Sports announcers connotatively use synonyms for the word *beat* to vary their reports of one team's victory over another. Consider, for instance, the connotative differences in these synonyms for *beat:*

John Q. University *beat* Alfred & William College

downed	whipped
nipped	thrashed
upset	drubbed
clobbered	kayoed
outlasted	pummeled
overcame	edged
put away	ruined
defeated	destroyed

Finally, notice the skillful use of connotation in this oral paragraph, taken from Bartolomeo Vanzetti's "Last Speech to the Court." Vanzetti, who along with Nicola Sacco was executed for murder on August 23, 1927, is describing and praising his friend, Sacco:

> I have talk a great deal of myself but I even forgot to name Sacco. Sacco too is a worker from his boyhood, a skilled worker lover of work, with a good job and pay, a good and lovely wife, two beautiful children and a neat little home at the verge of a wood, near a brook. Sacco is a heart, a faith, a character, a man; a man lover of nature and of mankind. A man who gave all, who sacrifice all to the cause of Liberty and to his love for mankind; money, rest, mundane ambitions, his own wife, his children, himself and his own life. Sacco has never dreamt to steal, never to assassinate. He and I have never brought a morsel of bread to our mouths, from our childhood to today—which has not been gained by the sweat of our brows. Never.

The same thing could have been said less connotatively, but with less sparkle. For instance, instead of saying, "He and I have never brought a morsel of bread to our mouths, from our childhood to today—which has not been gained by the sweat of our brows," the less sensitive speaker might have made the less connotative and more matter-of-fact assertion: "He and I always worked hard for a living—and never got anything for nothing."

ORAL SENTENCES

Perhaps there was a time when writers wrote like speakers talked. But if so, that time is long gone. Many writers nowadays write with all the force and complexity that come from having words mummified on a page. Some monster sentences on the page have gone beyond 4,000 words. *Absalom, Absalom,* a novel by William Faulkner, has a sentence of 1,300 words. The *Guinness Book of World Records* lists a record sentence containing 4,284 words that appeared in the *Report of the President of Columbia University, 1942–1943.* Listeners would surely walk away rather than endure such a barrage.

There are compelling reasons why speakers should compose their sentences altogether differently from writers, and throughout this book we have enumerated many of them. The chief reason, however, is simply this: Listeners cannot understand propositions that are worded in long, complex sentences. Readers can pause to track a wayward verb back to its subject, painstakingly stitch clauses together, and leisurely reconstruct the muddled sentences of a writer. But listeners have neither the time nor the opportunity to do this sort of reconstruction. If listeners fail to get a speaker's meaning on first hearing, the meaning is altogether lost to them.

Some written sentences border on the unintelligible no matter how often reread. The traditional sentence style of banks and other business institutions is monstrously complex and impossible to fathom. Many banks have lately recognized that their contracts are incomprehensible to the world at large and have begun to rewrite them. Here, for instance, is a passage from the old loan contract of a bank. Just for fun, read it aloud to a classmate:

> In the event of default in the payment of this or any other Obligation or the performance or observance of any term or covenant contained herein or in any note or other contract or agreement evidencing or relating to any Obligation or any Collateral on the Borrower's part to be performed or observed; or the undersigned Borrower shall die; or any of the undersigned become insolvent or make an assignment for the benefit of creditors; or a petition shall be filed by or against any of the undersigned under any provision of the Bankruptcy Act; or any money, securities or property of the undersigned now or hereafter on deposit with or in possession or under the control of the Bank shall be attached or become subject to distraint proceedings or any order or process of any court.

What does it all mean? Here is the same provision as stated in the new loan contract:

> I'll be in default:
> 1. If I don't pay an installment on time; or
> 2. If any other creditor tries by legal process to take any money of mine in your possession.

The second version contains the sentence style that students should studiously aim for. This style can be achieved if the following guidelines are observed.

Keep subjects close to verbs

If subjects and verbs are kept close together, the intelligibility of sentences is vastly increased. Ordinarily, when we talk, we tend to naturally keep our subjects close to their verbs.

> 1. <u>John</u> <u>went</u> to town.
>
> 2. The *<u>Titanic</u>* <u>was</u> a large ship of wonderful proportions.
>
> 3. <u>Smoke</u> <u>paralyzes</u> the cilia and causes them to stop beating.

The underlined words are subjects and verbs. Notice that in every case the one follows closely behind the other, making for instantly intelligible constructions.

Under the pressure of the moment, however, many speakers tend to become parenthetical. Clauses, phrases, and appositives are wantonly inserted between subject and verb, causing a dislocation in the natural subject-verb order and making the sentence more difficult to understand.

> 1. <u>John,</u> who wore a frayed winter coat and who last year had gone out for track but failed to make the team, <u>went</u> to town.
>
> 2. The *<u>Titanic,</u>* fantastically conceived, beautifully engineered, magnificently decorated, <u>was</u> a ship of wonderful proportions.
>
> 3. <u>Smoke,</u> which leaves the burning zone of the cigarette at 884°C, <u>paralyzes</u> the cilia and causes them to stop beating.

If you read these three sentences aloud, you will quickly see how much more difficult they are to understand than the first three, where subjects and verbs were kept close together. These same ideas could have been more intelligibly put, if they had been stated as separate sentences:

1. John went to town. He wore a frayed winter coat. Last year, he had gone out for track but failed to make the team.

2. The *Titanic* was fantastically conceived, beautifully engineered, and magnificently decorated. She was a ship of wonderful proportions.

3. Smoke leaves the burning zone of the cigarette at 884°C. It paralyzes the cilia and causes them to stop beating.

Use short and simple subjects

Sociologists and bureaucrats are fond of constructing sentences with serpentine subjects. These subjects are generally hammered out of a succession of nouns and noun phrases.

The implementation of the Safety at Sea Act that followed the sinking of the *Titanic* required all ships to carry enough lifeboats for their passengers.

The underlined words make up the subject of the sentence. Substitution by a pronoun—the standard test for identifying a subject—is possible:

It required all ships to carry enough lifeboats for their passengers.

What required?

The implementation of the Safety at Sea Act that followed the sinking of the *Titanic*.

This kind of construction, with a long, complex subject, is tediously difficult to understand. Listeners must hang giddily onto the subject as it slowly unravels, then quickly attach it to its verb. It is better to have two sentences:

Following the sinking of the *Titanic,* the Safety at Sea Act was implemented. This act required all ships to carry enough lifeboats for their passengers.

Use short and moderately short sentences

Long sentences are difficult for listeners to follow and hard for speakers to say. The information in a long sentence is often divided on the page by commas, dashes, and brackets. Punctuation marks, however, are invisible to listeners and, in a speech, must be signaled by the speaker's voice. It is simply asking too much of listeners to expect them to follow a long sentence as well as a complex series of punctuation marks heard only through oral clues. Consider this sentence, taken from a biography of Geoffrey Chaucer:

> Even in a fairly large city like London—a mere town by comparison to modern London, though swarming with people packed together in small apartments like chickens in market crates—most people lived out their lives in neighborhoods, tannery workers associating primarily with tannery workers (and the hawkers or stallkeepers who sold them their fruit and vegetables, their pots and pans and the makings for their brooms), wine people associating mostly with wine people, rich men associating mostly with rich men who attended the same parties or lodged next door, safe in the more comfortable sections of their specialized business districts, in great, sober houses to which the successful, with their servants and apprentices, fled from the noise, stink, and crowding of the poor. . . .

Even Solomon would find this sentence impossible to follow if it was given in a speech.

Very much the same thing could be said in shorter sentences, and with greatly improved clarity. This is how a speaker could put the same ideas:

> By comparison to modern London, London was then a mere town. But even in such a large city, people lived with people, packed together in small apartments like chickens in market crates. Most people lived out their lives in neighborhoods. Tan-

nery workers associated with tannery workers and with the hawkers or stallkeepers from whom they bought their fruits and vegetables, their pots and pans and the makings for their brooms. Wine people associated mostly with wine people. Rich men associated mostly with rich men who attended the same parties or lodged next door. The rich lived safe in the more comfortable sections of their specialized business districts. They occupied great, sober houses, to which they fled with their servants and apprentices to avoid the noise, stink, and crowding of the poor. . . .

The point is not to talk in short, childish sentences, like characters from some absurdist play, but to talk in sentences varied enough to be interesting yet short enough to be instantly understood.

Don't use inverted sentences

Writers sometimes invert the parts of a sentence either for emphasis, variety, or some other effect. Such constructions, while they may be stylish and eye-catching on the page, are difficult for listeners to understand. Here is an example:

Awkward: That smoking causes lung cancer, coronary artery diseases, chronic bronchitis, and emphysema, were the irrefutable findings of the Surgeon General.

Speakers would not utter such a sentence naturally. Here is the same sentence, but in normal word order:

Better: The irrefutable findings of the Surgeon General were that smoking causes lung cancer, coronary artery diseases, chronic bronchitis, and emphysema.

Generally speaking, you are better off avoiding such inverted constructions in speech. If you feel compelled to invert an occasional sentence, invert only short sentences, and only for emphasis. Instead of saying:

The *Titanic* went down to her watery grave.

you could say:

Down to her watery grave went the *Titanic*.

Don't accumulate initial clauses

Sentences that bristle with initial clauses are more characteristically found in writing than in speeches. Such sentences are easy to read but difficult to listen to. Here is an example:

Awkward: His use of drums, his use of horns where before only violins dared to venture, his swelling, flashy rolls of the piano, his bold almost brassy renderings of themes, these were the distinctive stamps of genius that characterized the music of Beethoven.

It is possible for listeners to follow such utterances, but only with great patience and care. Better to state the same ideas more plainly:

Better: Beethoven's music bore distinctive stamps of genius. His use of drums and horns was wholly original. His music was characterized by flashy, swelling rolls of the piano, and bold, almost brassy rendering of themes.

Use the active voice

Speakers use the active voice almost instinctively. It is far commoner for a speaker to say:

I vividly remember my last trip to England.

than to say:

My last trip to England is vividly remembered by me.

Under certain conditions, writing the passive voice is justified. Scientific papers, for instance, are usually written in the passive voice to invest their findings with a kind of subjectless universality. Speakers, however, are better off using the active voice. Sentences written in the active voice—the more familiar oral construction—are easier to understand; moreover, sentences spoken in the active voice sound friendlier and less pompous. Instead of saying something like:

A number of geophysical and biological processes are known in which carbon monoxide is produced.

say:

Carbon monoxide is produced by a number of known geophysical and biological processes.

In sum, when composing a speech, you should draft sentences that are easy to say. Read the sentences out loud. If they don't sound like something you would naturally say, rewrite them until they do. Remember that oral sentences should be more casual and informal than sentences that are written for an essay or term paper. Prepositions should occur at the end of the sentence, if that's where they would naturally go. Don't say, "This is the sort of work for which he was fitted." Instead, say "This is the sort of work he was fitted for." Use contractions like "don't," "aren't," and "won't" even if you wouldn't use them in writing. Avoid stilted and literary phrases such as "It must be borne in mind," or "With reference to." Address your audience as "you." Finally, bear these numbers in mind, courtesy of readibility expert Rudolf Flesch, who says that a seventeen-word sentence is standard; a twenty-one-word sentence is fairly difficult; a twenty-five-word sentence is difficult; and a twenty-nine or more word sentence is very difficult. Though they refer to the readability of sentences, these figures nevertheless can give you an idea of how difficult your sentences might be to a listener.

EXERCISES

1. Pick out the more concrete word from the following pairs of words:

expenses	pisces	Geronimo
food bills	astrological signs	Indian
ulcer	dictionary	paper
sickness	book	foolscap
prisons	sailboats	biplanes
institutions	ketch	airplanes
science	short story	bird
chemistry	fiction	sparrow

2. Correct any word usage problems you find in the following sentences:

   a. The pallid pallbearer poked his head into the parlor.
   b. The *Titanic* was a gigantic ship.
   c. He asked us to follow into the hollow of the hills.
   d. Sloppy, slatternly speech often characterizes their exchanges.

3. From the following pairs of words, choose the one whose connotative meaning fits better with the rest of the sentence:

   a. The lame beggar (hobbled, sauntered) through the doorway.

   b. She gave a wicked smile and cocked her eyebrows in an expression of arch (enjoyment, amusement).

   c. His contemptuous attitude has (buffaloed, alienated) many of his friends.

   d. Grieving, the widow and her children made their way (ponderously, solemnly) through the cemetery.

   e. He told her wicked lies, adding (contrivance, deception) to his other offenses.

4. Rewrite the following sentences to make them easier for listeners to understand:

   a. Howard Richards, whose book *They Shall Inherit the Earth* is a damning indictment of the carelessness with which our highest institutions have administered their public trust, was of a contrary opinion.

   b. The administration of the cafeteria finances by the Central Student Committee has resulted in many unnecessary expenses.

   c. John Chaucer was "a citizen of London," as he was proud to say, a rich and influential vintner—which is roughly the fourteenth-century equivalent of the modern large brewer in Ireland or England, though John Chaucer was not by any means a personage up to the enormous wealth and power of, say, the Busch family of St. Louis or the greater beermeisters of Germany, men more nearly comparable with fourteenth-century barons.

   d. That the city council is derelict of its duty, that it should be subjected to an immediate recall vote, is evident from its dismal failure to find an answer to the sewer problem.

   e. While the FDA is responsible for the purity of our food, the efficacy and safety of our drugs, and the hygienic standards of food processors, it is not responsible for running our private lives.

NOTES

[1] Chief Joseph of the Nez Perce Tribe, "Surrender Speech."

CHAPTER  **10**

Practicing speech delivery

Speak clearly, if you speak at all.
—Oliver Wendell Holmes

THE SPEAKER'S VOICE

Do you think you have good speech delivery? Try reading this paragraph from a standard test given to applicants for jobs as radio announcers:

> I bought a batch of baking powder and baked a batch of biscuits. I brought a big basket of biscuits back to the bakery and baked a basket of big biscuits. Then I took the big basket of biscuits and the basket of big biscuits and mixed the big biscuits with the basket of biscuits that was next to the big basket and put a bunch of biscuits from the basket into a box. Then I took the box of mixed biscuits and a biscuit mixer and brought the basket of biscuits and the box of mixed biscuits and the biscuit mixer to the bakery and opened a tin of sardines.

Chances are you didn't get past the first "big basket of biscuits."

"To slur is human," said John Mason Brown. Many of us not only slur, we mumble, chew our words, or spit them out like seeds. Some of us talk through our noses; some of us swallow our words. "Americans," according to one speech authority, "are best known for having the worst articulation in the Western world."[1]

The principal aim of all speech is intelligibility. We talk not just to be heard, but to be understood. Intelligibility is a variable quality. Some speakers are clear, crisp, and instantly understandable; others slur their words, mumble, or talk too fast to be intelligible. Still other speakers cannot articulate certain sounds. The cartoon character Elmer Fudd, for instance, missays his "r's" as "w's"—a speech characteristic shared by newscaster Barbara Walters.

What do listeners deduce about a speaker from his or her voice? They deduce a surprising amount of information, although some of it is of dubious accuracy. Studies have found that listeners tend to judge the status and credibility of a speaker from the speaker's voice.[2] Use a flat tone of voice, and listeners will judge you cold and withdrawn; use a nasal tone, and they will find you repugnant. Speak in a high pitched voice, and you'll be judged as effeminate; speak at a rapid rate, and you'll be seen as enthusiastic.[3] Indeed, the way you talk even has an effect on your employability, especially if you are looking for a clerical or technical position.[4] "There is no index of character so sure as the human voice," said British parliamentarian Benjamin Disraeli. Apparently many people believe that.

THE PSYCHOLOGY OF SPEECH DELIVERY

Students in speech classes are often unsure about how they should behave when they give speeches. Some play the "orator"; others play the "anti-orator." One student in giving a middling speech on "The Lamaze Method of Natural Childbirth" got up to the podium, squared her shoulders, and looked her audience straight in the face. Giving the back row a broad wink, she puffed herself up and began declaiming as though she were an evangelist speaking to throngs in the Astrodome. When she was done, she repeated the wink to the back row, drawing a titter, and resumed her seat.

A second student behaved in exactly the opposite way—playing the part of the "anti-orator." He slouched to the podium, stared morosely at his shoe, and began to mumble. The students in the back row protested that they couldn't hear him. He raised his voice, stared defiantly at the students, and continued with the speech. As soon as he was done, he scampered back to his seat, breathing a loud sigh of relief.

The occasion of giving a speech before a classroom of their peers causes student speakers varying degrees of discomfort. All classes require students to produce, but usually in private transactions involving only the student and teacher. English classes require students to write papers; chemistry classes require students to do experiments. But neither the papers nor the experiments are ever seen by anyone other than the teacher. In speech classes, however, students are required to produce visibly and publicly—to get up before both students and teacher and give a speech.

Although in-class speechmaking may initially cause you to be uncomfortable, perhaps it would help if you knew more or less what teachers and audiences expect from student speeches. First of all, most teachers expect students to give speeches but not to playact at doing them. The ideal is to speak and behave as if you're holding an extended conversation with yourself. Speak loudly enough to be heard, casually enough to be pleasant, and naturally enough to be yourself. Don't put on airs or puff yourself up with oratorical self-importance. Emphasize your points with gestures, but not to a silly excess.

Second, most teachers—as well as most educated audiences—prefer content to posturing, reason to hysterics, and logic to claptrap. The vast majority of teachers are rather kindly disposed toward student speeches and are about as forgiving of errors as you would be of the conversational manners of a friend. You needn't, therefore, try to be especially dramatic or rousing in your delivery. Instead, if you manage to be audible, reasonable, and intelligible, your speech will most likely be a success.

Finally, teachers do not expect students to adopt a special language or delivery style just for the purpose of giving a speech. Good delivery is neither cute nor noticeable. Like tact, good delivery is a trait whose presence is never detected, but whose absence is glaringly obvious. Preserve your own way of talking when you give a speech (that is, of course, so long as your natural manner of speaking is understandable). Retain your own characteristic gestures; use the same pauses and emphases in the speech as you would in a one-to-one conversation. Rather than acting the part of someone else as you deliver the speech, you should concentrate on serving up a heightened form of the real "you."

THE PHYSIOLOGY OF SPEECH DELIVERY

Sound travels in pressure waves that are detected by the ear drum, transmitted to some 30,000 nerve fibers in the inner ear, and relayed as electrical impulses to the brain for interpretation. Basically, this is the process by which we hear voices. We hear our own voices through the skull bones, which amplify the vibrations in our vocal chords and cause us to sound louder to ourselves than we do to others. Sound waves, much like the ripples made by a stone thrown into a still pond, are intensest near the source of the sound and gradually diminish in intensity as the sound travels farther away. Moreover, sound waves are blotted out by background noise and absorbed by capacious surroundings. If you are in a noisy room, or a massive auditorium, you have to speak louder to be heard.

The following are other characteristics of the human voice.

Volume

Volume—the loudness of sound—is measured in decibels. A whisper from about four feet away measures 20 decibels; faint speech occurs at about 40 decibels; an ordinary conversation from a distance of three feet takes place at between 55–66 decibels.

Whether or not a speaker is talking loud enough to be heard varies with at least two factors. The first is the amount of background noise. The background noise of an empty theatre is about 25 decibels; of the average home, about 32 decibels; of a noisy restaurant, about 70 decibels. To be understood in these environments, speakers must talk above the decibel level of the background noise. The distance of a listener from the speaker is a second factor affecting whether or not the speaker can be heard. Imagine that there are five rows of toy boats floating in a bathtub and that a pebble is tossed in front of the first row. Waves from the pebble will cause the first row of boats to vigorously bob up and down, the second less so, the third even less, and the fifth least of all. Sound waves have a similar effect on rows of listeners. The waves diminish in intensity as they ripple away from their source. Listeners in the row nearest to the speaker receive the sound waves in greatest intensity; listeners farther away receive them in least intensity and consequently do not hear the speaker as clearly.

Volume is a prime factor in a speaker's intelligibility. If you don't talk loud enough, listeners will neither hear you nor understand you. Bear in mind, as mentioned earlier, that your own voice, because it is amplified by the bones of your skull, sounds louder to you than to a listener. To be sure you're talking loud enough, look at listeners in the back row. If you see them craning forward, cupping their hands to their ears, or looking disgruntled and bored, you're probably not talking loud enough.

Pitch

Pitch refers to the relative highness or lowness of sounds. Different sounds are heard at a different pitch. The buzz of a bee, for instance, is heard at a lower pitch, while the squeak of a mouse is heard at a higher pitch. Sounds differ in pitch because sound waves differ in frequencies. The thirty thousand nerve fibers in the inner ear are stimulated by, and tuned to detect, sounds of different frequencies that are heard at a different pitch. Audiologists measure hearing on a scale that ranges from a low to a high pitch. Hearing loss can occur at one end of the scale without affecting a person's ability to hear sounds at the other.

The customary pitch at which a person generally speaks is said to be the key of his or her voice. Men generally speak at a lower pitch than women. A study indicated that a higher pitch in a man's voice is generally perceived as a sign of either a dynamic, feminine, or artistically inclined personality. However, women who speak at a higher pitch are perceived by their listeners as dynamic and extroverted.[5]

No skilled speaker would address an audience in a monotone—with no change in voice inflection or pitch. We all have a pitch range, which we use to emotionally color our utterances. Consider, for instance, the word *you* spoken with various pitch inflections.

said with a rapidly rising pitch, implies a different emotion (Is it really you!) than spoken with a falling pitch (Not you, again!)

The first *you* indicates pleasure, excitement, and surprise at seeing someone; the second *you* implies displeasure and disappointment. The same word spoken as a flat monotone Y o u expresses a third reaction (Oh, it's only you). Speakers modulate pitch to animate their words and sentences and to imply something of how they feel. Pitch change for emotional coloring, however, is seldom premeditatedly done except by actors plying their craft. We don't pause in midsentence and meditate on what pitch to use on the next word. Instead, most of us change pitch naturally and unconsciously, depending on how we feel at the moment.

Rate

Rate is the speed at which a speaker talks. Normal rate of speech varies from between 140 to 180 words per minute, depending on whether a speaker is calm, tense, angry, or agitated. When we are angry or excited, we tend to speak faster; when we are depressed or subdued, we tend to speak at a slower rate.

Rate of speech has an obvious and immediate effect on a speaker's intelligibility. Some speakers talk at a dizzying rate, reeling off words and sentences in an unintelligible jumble. Student speakers, especially when they are suffering from speechfright, are often guilty of talking too fast. The contrary mistake—of talking too slowly—is rarer but just as likely to affect intelligibility. Listeners who must wait an interminable time for a speaker to complete a sentence are likely to stop listening and start daydreaming. Cowpokes on the backs of horses may sound romantic when they drawl, but speakers on the fronts of podiums soon begin to seem merely boring.

Articulation

Articulation is the sound-producing process by which we utter clear, distinct syllables. Students generally confuse articulation with pronunciation. Some dictionaries, in fact, list the two words as synonyms. But articulation and pronunciation refer to different aspects of the speechmaking process. Pronunciation is the way that individual words should be uttered. For instance, the correct pronunciation of the word "fable" is listed in *Webster's New World Dictionary* this way: fā'b'l. The vowel *a* is elongated; the *e* at the end of the word is silent. Articulation refers to the manner in which speakers say vowels and consonants. Some speakers chronically slur their words, blithely ignoring the dictionary guide to pronunciation. Other speakers are unrepentant clippers who snip syllables off every word they utter. In sum, pronunciation refers to the way individual words should be spoken; articulation refers to the way individual speakers say various words. Here in an imaginary exchange between two fishermen is articulation at its very worst:

When Fishermen Meet

Hyamac.   Lobuddy.

Binearlong?   Coplours.

Cetchenenny?	Goddafew.
Kinarthy?	Bassencarp.
Enysiztoom?	Coplapounds.
Hittenhard?	Sordalike.
Fishinonabodem?	Rytonabodem.
Watchaadrinkin?	Jugojimbeam.
Igoddago.	Tubad.
Seeyaroun.	Yetekedezy.
Guluk.	

Poor articulation is a prime cause of speaker unintelligibility. The more distinctly you utter your vowels and consonants, the easier you are to understand. The more you mumble, clip, snip, slur, or chew your words, the less intelligible you become. Some speakers have articulation problems caused by a speech defect. But for the majority of healthy mumblers, poor articulation is caused by bad speech habits. Most of us mumble and gobble our words in casual talks with our friends; our friends likewise return the favor by mumbling and gobbling to us. We are as benignly forgiving of their articulation as they are of ours. Gobbling and mumbling, in fact, constitute a kind of speech norm when friends casually meet. But it is a corrupting norm that, if not counteracted by exposure to more formal speech occasions requiring distinct articulation, will quickly infect our way of speaking. Chronic articulation problems—even a bad case of slurring—are not easily overcome. If you don't articulate well, consult with your teacher. Various articulatory exercises exist, which, if conscientiously practiced, can help the slurrer.

ADAPTING SPEECH DELIVERY TO THE OCCASION

"The sound must seem an echo to the sense," wrote the English poet Alexander Pope. He was referring to the use of rhyme and rhythm in poetry. Pope's maxim also applies to speech delivery. Adjustments must be made in delivery depending on the speech occasion. It is inconceivable, for instance, that a speaker would use the same style of delivery at a wake as at a wedding. Some variables of delivery are adjustable on demand; others are not. For example, you cannot drastically alter the quality of your voice to suit every occasion. But you can talk either softer or louder, slow down the rate of your speech, and use fewer gestures. In sum, it is possible to modify your delivery to match the occasion for speechmaking.

Appropriateness is the cardinal rule to be observed in making adjustments in speech delivery. To paraphrase Pope, "The delivery must seem an echo to the sense." Or, to put it more prosaically, the delivery style must be appropriate to the content and occasion of the speech. It is simply a matter of common sense—how you should deliver the speech—the same sort of common sense you would use in deciding how to recite a poem. These lines, for instance:

> Rats!
> They fought the dogs and killed the cats,
> And bit the babies in the cradles,
> And ate the cheeses out of the vats,
> And licked the soups from the cooks' own ladles,
> Split open kegs of salted sprats,
> Made nests inside men's Sunday hats,
> And even spoiled the women's chats,
> By drowning their speaking
> With shrieking and squeaking
> In fifty different sharps and flats.
> —Robert Browning,
> *The Pied Piper of Hamlin*

obviously cry out for a different recital style than these lines:

> Break, break, break,
> On thy cold gray stones, O Sea!
> And I would that my tongue could utter
> The thoughts that arise in me.
> —Alfred, Lord Tennyson,
> *Break, Break, Break*

The differences in these stanzas call for obvious delivery and interpretative adjustments in a reciter. Differing occasions of speechmaking likewise require speakers to adjust their styles of delivery.

Speaking oral paragraphs

A written paragraph is identified on the page by a visible indentation; an oral paragraph is identified by the way it is spoken. Listeners have no other clues to the procession of oral paragraphs except in the enunciation emphases provided by a speaker's voice. Oral paragraphs should therefore be spoken as separate units of thought in the speech, much as a reciter would speak the different stanzas of a poem. Below are some guidelines to help you speak coherent and understandable oral paragraphs.

Pause at the end of an oral paragraph   Listeners have no way of knowing when a paragraph has ended unless you so indicate with a pause. The pause allows listeners to digest what has just been said and to anticipate what is about to come. Moreover, it signals to them the end of one idea and the introduction of another.

Emphasize the generalization of the oral paragraph   Such emphasis is achieved through proper enunciation of the generalization—the single most important idea of the paragraph—and the idea that the paragraph should amplify and develop. If listeners mishear the generalization of a paragraph, the supporting details will be meaningless to them.

Emphasize transition from one paragraph to another   Following the pause that signals the end of a paragraph, you should emphasize any transitional words or phrases such as *moreover, however, but, nevertheless,* which signal the movement of the speech from one paragraph to another. With this sort of emphasis provided, listeners will be better able to track the development of a speech through a succession of oral paragraphs.

Finally, in delivering the speech you should not resort to a predictable or singsong way of emphasizing its oral paragraphs. Use gestures and variations in volume, rate, and pitch to emphasize the movement of the speech from one paragraph to another. But don't successively use the same gestures and the same variations, or your speech will sound as though it were being delivered by a robot.

NOTES

[1] Brigance, William Norwood. *Speech: Its Techniques and Disciplines in a Free Society.* New York: Appleton-Century-Crofts, 1961.

[2] Harms, L. S. "Listener Judgments of Status Cues in Speech." *Quarterly Journal of Speech,* (April 1961), pp. 164–68.

[3] Addington, David W. "The Relationship of Selected Vocal Characteristics to Personality Perception." *Speech Monographs,* XXXV (Nov. 1968), pp. 492–503.

[4] Hopper, Robert and Frederick Williams. "Speech Characteristics and Employability." *Speech Monographs* XL (Nov. 1973), pp. 296–302.

[5] Addington, p. 502.

Revising the speech

. . . Nobody ever admired an orator for correct grammar; they only laugh at him if his grammar is bad . . .

—Cicero

HOW TO REVISE YOUR SPEECH

The differences between the language styles of writers and speakers have been repeatedly emphasized throughout this text. We have pointed out that, for the most part, an oral paragraph is more repetitious than a written paragraph, an oral sentence is more instantly intelligible than a written sentence, and an oral vocabulary is more colloquial than a written vocabulary. "Does it read well?" remarked British parliamentarian Charles Fox. "Then it's not a good speech." No doubt his was an exaggerated and biased view. Some good speeches do read well; some do not. But all good speeches appeal as much to the ear as to the eye.

Because of the differences between writing and speaking, a speech should be revised not only on the page but, principally, in the utterance. You should tinker with the speech only after enunciating it out loud. Ask a friend to be your critic by sitting in the back row, listening to your speech, and making suggestions about improving it. If you cannot get a friend to help you, use a tape recorder to monitor the way your speech sounds. In sum, make all revisions on the basis of how the speech sounds when given out loud, not on how it reads on the page.

Checklist

To help you with the revision of your speech, in this chapter we condense information and advice given in earlier chapters about various parts of the speech. Make your revisions by systematically following the checklist below and going over your speech for the flaws and weaknesses noted under each heading.

Check the structure of the speech   Folk wisdom tells us that some people cannot see the forest because of the trees. Indeed, it is a rather common blunder to become so engrossed with the individual words, sentences, and paragraphs of a speech that some obvious defect in the structure of the speech itself is overlooked. Check, therefore, the text of the speech against the outline to be sure that in the heat of composing you didn't stray from the central idea of the speech or deal lopsidedly with its various topics. Here, for instance, is an outline that, if followed, would result in a lopsided treatment of the topics in the central idea:

Central idea: The police have two different roles: the criminal and the noncriminal role.

    I. The criminal role

   II. The noncriminal role
      A. Traffic control
      B. Personal counseling
      C. Providing information

Such structural defects are more easily spotted in an outline than in a speech.

In drafting the speech, it is more than likely that you have deviated somewhat from the outline. If so, make a new outline of the speech as you have written it, and check it for digressions or lopsidedness. Bear in mind that the sequence of topics in the speech should conform to the sequence announced in the central idea. If the central idea promises to deal first with the criminal role of the police and then with the noncriminal role, that is the order of presentation that should be followed in the speech. Consistency of this sort makes the speech easier for an audience to follow. For more discussion on the kinds of structural defects to look for in a speech, review Chapter 7.

Check the wording of the central idea   Of all the ideas contained in a speech, the central idea should be the most clearly and emphatically worded and the most distinctly enunciated. The central idea is to the speech what a foundation is to a building. Some commonsense notions about the central idea are given in Chapter 4, which you should now take time out to review. Be especially certain that the central idea sums up the main contentions of the speech, and that the body of the speech reinforces and develops the main points of the central idea.

Check the wording of the introductory paragraph   Speeches, like chess games, prosper from good openings. Many listeners sound out a speech from its first paragraph and make the decision there and then to snooze or not to snooze. Various openings can be used to jolt awake the would-be snoozers and hold their interest. You could begin with a shocking announcement or remark. Here is a classic example of the use of this tactic:

> Henry Ward Beecher had a genius for bringing the most somnolent audience to life. One July morning he rode into a West Virginia town which was widely known in lecture circles as "Death Valley"—for the reason that any speaker unfortunate enough to have an engagement to lecture there wilted and curled up when he faced the town's stupid and indifferent audience.
>
> Beecher was duly warned. That afternoon, when he was being introduced, half the audience was already dozing. Beecher rose from his chair and, wiping his brow with a large handkerchief, strode to the front of the platform.
>
> "It's a God-damned hot day," the clergyman began.
>
> A thousand pairs of eyes goggled and an electrical shock straightened the crowd erect. Beecher paused, and then, raising a finger of solemn reproof, went on, "That's what I heard a man say here this afternoon!"
>
> He then proceeded into a stirring condemnation of blasphemy and, needless to say, took the audience with him.

You could also begin the speech *in medias res* (in the middle of things) like the ancient Greek poets, who always began their epics right in the thick of things—a battle, a quarrel, or some other such stirring event. Here is an example of a speech that opens *in medias res:*

> And Allen had of course arrived—as the law required—escorted by one (or both) parent (parents) not as the law required, but as the officer suggested. He had no personal belongings with him, not that they were forbidden—he just didn't have any. He had a coat; he had part of a coat (the rips and tears secured with safety pins and high hopes). And his shoes were worn through and stuffed with cardboard—not that it would matter in there. Even looking at the building frightened him; the bars, the screened-in windows, and locked doors, the people inside he had never seen (but had heard of) who were strict and cold, generous only in the distribution of punishment and the resurrection of easily forgotten rules. The door opened. He went in. And Allen began his first day at school.[1]

It is impossible to give an exact prescription for the kind of opening to use for a speech. It depends on what your speech is about, and what your audience is like. Generally speaking, you should use the opening paragraph to win the audience's interest and to state the central idea. If the opening paragraph of your speech, instead of orienting the audience, immediately begins to smother them with mounds of technical matter, you should rewrite it. Audiences will be more kindly disposed toward you and more manageable when gently led to the heart of a subject.

Check the wording of the oral paragraphs   Oral paragraphs should be checked for unity, coherence, and emphasis. Ask your listener/friend to give an opinion on each paragraph after you have uttered it. Check the generalization in each paragraph for clarity and force of expression. Be sure that each generalization is adequately developed and amplified by supporting details. To this end, you should review chapters 5 and 8.

Oral paragraph transitions, external and internal, should be checked. If the speech seems to lurch abruptly from one paragraph to another, you should insert more external transitions between the paragraphs. If the discussion within individual paragraphs seems rough and uneven, more internal transitions are probably needed. You should be sure to also check paragraphs for their orality—the ease with which they can be spoken and instantly understood. Bear in mind that oral paragraphs are generally more repetitious and redundant than written paragraphs. If any point within a paragraph seems cryptic or unclear to your listener, use repetition and restatement to clarify it.

Check the diction of the speech   Diction refers to the individual words that make up the speech. Reread Chapter 9, *Wording the Speech,* for advice on word usage. Be especially careful about the use of unfamiliar, sesquipedalian words such as *sesquipedalian*—merely another word for very long. Use a colloquial vocabulary—the sort of words and expressions that occur naturally when you're talking. Rewrite any cacophonous combinations or any obvious internal rhymes.

Check the sentence structure of the speech   In the wording of the speech sentences, you should aim for instant intelligibility. Long, involved, twisted sentences should be rewritten to be shorter, more understandable units. Check for awkward placement of verbs and nouns; for overuse of long, cumbersome subjects; for use of complex inverted constructions that are difficult to understand. It is best to check all sentences as you speak them. Ask your friend / listener how any dubious sentence sounds. Ask yourself whether or not you would speak the sentence in conversation with a friend. If the answer is "no," rewrite the sentence.

Check the final paragraph for closure   In his famous poem, *The Hollow Men,* T. S. Eliot penned a well-known line about the world ending "not with a bang but a whimper." A similar end threatens many speeches.

As with introductory paragraphs, there are various tactics for constructing final paragraphs, but all final paragraphs should be characterized by *closure*—a sense of having come to a logical and expected end. Some final paragraphs achieve closure by restating or summarizing what has been already said in the body of the speech. Some end by drawing conclusions, or proposing a course of action. Here, for instance, in a satirical speech titled "Advice to Youth," Mark Twain ends by drawing an unexpected conclusion. In the speech, he has dispensed tongue-in-cheek advice to his youthful audience, urging them to obey their parents when the parents are present, to hit disrespectful strangers with a brick, and to lie carefully so as not to get caught.

> But I have said enough. I hope you will treasure up the instructions which I have given you, and make them a guide to your feet

and a light to your understanding. Build your character thoughtfully and painstakingly upon these precepts, and by and by, when you have got it built, you will be surprised and gratified to see how nicely and sharply it resembles everybody else's.

In sum, final paragraphs should end with more bang than whimper. State your conclusions; give your suggestions; draw your inferences. Do so positively and forcefully and the speech will seem to naturally and logically come to an end.

Check your delivery for vocal emphasis   Practice and refine your delivery before your friendly listener, experimenting with vocal emphasis until you are satisfied. Remember to enunciate oral paragraphs as separate units, to mark their beginning and end with pauses, and to duly emphasize their generalizations. For further suggestions on delivery, review Chapter 10.

Once you have practiced the speech and refined your delivery of it, you can mark cues to yourself on the manuscript. Underlining, for instance, can be used to indicate vocal emphasis of some sentence or passage; arrows or other marks can be used to indicate pauses. Cue yourself on the manuscript with any other delivery instructions.

Finally, though no universal blueprint for revising a speech can be given other than the general advice of this chapter, students who try in their revisions to make their speeches clearer and more "talkable" cannot go wrong.

NOTES

[1] Patricia Warren, "Bring Forth the Children," Interstate Oratorical Association, 1971.

3

GENERAL
TYPES
OF SPEECHES

CHAPTER

The speech to inform

New things are made familiar, and familiar things are made new.

—Alexander Pope

DEFINITION OF THE SPEECH TO INFORM

The word *inform* comes from the Latin *informare,* meaning "to give form to, shape, fashion from an idea, describe." This is the sense that the sixteenth-century poet Edmund Spenser had in mind when he wrote: "Infinite shapes of creatures / *Informed* in the mud on which the Sunne hath shyned." But such a meaning is not the prevailing sense of the word. Nowadays *inform* means to "impart knowledge of some particular fact or occurrence to a person." William II of Normandy had this modern sense in mind when he wrote, "Ascham *informs* us that Elizabeth understood Greek. . . ." This excursion into etymology tells us what students who give a speech to inform must do: They must give shape and form to a speech; they must impart knowledge about something in it.

What is the informative speech? Basically, it is a speech whose primary purpose is to give information. We say primary because in speechmaking, as in most kinds of human activities, purity of purpose is a rarity. The informative speech principally intends to inform; but in the act of informing, it might also persuade or even entertain. Such effects, however, would be secondary to its primary purpose.

Speeches of this kind cover a vast number of topics, since even the simplest subject can usually be explained in a more detailed and informative way. The speech to inform can carry us through specific instructions, describe far-off cities and sights, explain ordinary or complex events. It can tell us how the bullfighter kills a bull, how a department store computes finance charges, or how we can change our names. Such speeches usually answer the simple interrogatives: who, what, when, where, how, or why.

ORAL PARAGRAPHS IN THE SPEECH TO INFORM

The basic molecule of any speech is the oral paragraph. The speech to inform is usually made up of oral paragraphs that define, describe, divide and classify, compare and contrast, explain process, and outline cause. Separate paragraphs are ordinarily devoted to each of these functions.

The oral paragraph that defines

A definition attempts to answer the most basic question an audience can have about an object: What is it? Definitions usually identify the category to which the item belongs and then show how the item differs from others in that category. Here are a few abbreviated examples of definitions:

> Chemistry is the science whose primary concern . . .
>
> Love is an emotion characterized by . . .
>
> An atomic clock is a method of keeping time that uses . . .

For the purpose of exemplifying, we have deliberately worded these abridged definitions to rather mechanically link the item to be defined with its category. More subtle and varied wordings are, of course, possible. In our examples, chemistry is linked to the category of science, love to emotion, and atomic clocks to methods of timekeeping. Once identified with a category, the item is then differentiated from others in the same category. Characteristics that differentiate chemistry from other sciences, love from other emotions, and atomic clocks from other methods of timekeeping therefore have to be detailed for the definitions to be complete. Here is an example. First, palimpsest is identified with the category of writing surfaces, and then it is differentiated from them:

> Palimpsest is a writing surface, whether of vellum, papyrus, or other material, which has been used twice or more for manuscript purposes. Before the invention of paper, the scarcity of writing material made such substances very valuable and the vellum surfaces were often scraped or rubbed or the papyrus surfaces washed. With material so used a second time it frequently happened that the earlier script either was not completely erased or that, with age, it showed through the new. In this way many documents of very early periods have been preserved for posterity.

Because objects and ideas are often named for their origins and functions, etymologies—explanations that trace the roots and histories of words—are often used in definitions. Here an etymological explanation is used to help define *botulism:*

> What is botulism? Botulism is poisoning caused by the toxin of the bacteria Clostridium botulinum. "Clostridium" is Latin for "little spindle," which is what the bacterium looks like under a microscope; "botulinum" comes from "botulus," the Latin word for sausage, the food in which the poison first made its appearance.

Such an explanation not only tells the audience how the organism got its name; it also tells something of the organism's looks and history.

Giving examples is another widely used method of defining. Examples can clarify the meaning of a term by citing applications of it. Here, for instance, in two paragraphs, psychiatrist Carl Rogers defines a technical term, *congruence,* with the aid of examples:

It has been found that personal change is facilitated when the psychotherapist is what *he* is, when in the relationship with his client he is genuine and without "front" or facade, openly being the feelings and attitudes which at the moment are flowing *in* him. We have coined the term "congruence" to try to describe this condition. By this we mean that the feelings the therapist is experiencing are available to him, available to his awareness, and he is able to live these feelings, be them, and able to communicate them if appropriate. No one fully achieves this condition, yet the more the therapist is able to listen acceptantly to what is going on within himself, and the more he is able to be the complexity of his feelings, without fear, the higher the degree of his congruence.

To give a commonplace example, each of us senses this quality in people in a variety of ways. One of the things which offends us about radio and TV commercials is that it is often perfectly evident from the tone of voice that the announcer is "putting on," playing a role, saying something he doesn't feel. This is an example of incongruence. On the other hand each of us knows individuals whom we somehow trust because we sense that they are being what they are, that we are dealing with the person himself, not with a polite or professional front. It is this quality of congruence which we sense which research has found to be associated with successful therapy. The more genuine and congruent the therapist in the relationship, the more probability there is that change in personality in the client will occur.[1]

Testimony from an authority is also frequently used in definitions, especially when the term to be defined is technical or controversial. Here is an example:

What is this thing called hemophilia? Webster defines it as "a tendency, usually hereditary, to profuse bleeding even from slight wounds." Dr. Armand J. Quick, Professor of Biochemistry at Marquette University and recognized world authority on this topic, defines it as "prothrombin consumption of 8 to 13 seconds." Normal time is 15 seconds. Now do you know what hemophilia is?[2]

Although they are found in a wide variety of speeches that have a variety of purposes, definitions are especially useful and necessary in the informative speech. But not all informative speeches contain oral paragraphs that define. The speech, for instance, on the composition of hot dogs (see page 74) made no attempt at definition simply because none was necessary. You should define only those words, phrases, or expressions whose meanings are ambiguous, controversial, technical, or abstract. You should not define ordinary and unambiguous terms such as hot dog, dictionary, or cowboy, but any term or word used in a special sense—for example, Rogers' use of the word *congruence*—should be defined. In sum, define as necessary to inform your audience on the subject of the speech.

The oral paragraph that describes

A definition tells; a description shows. Often in giving a speech that informs, it is necessary to both show and tell. Descriptive paragraphs, however, are not effective if they merely contain a catalog of adjectives. The most effective description assembles its adjectives under a *dominant impression*. As the term implies, the dominant impression is a principal characteristic of the thing to be described and forms the hub of the descriptive paragraph. Here are two paragraphs describing hell, taken from a sermon in James Joyce's *Portrait of the Artist As a Young Man,* which exemplify the use of a dominant impression:

> Hell is a strait and dark and foulsmelling prison, an abode of demons and lost souls, filled with fire and smoke. The straitness of this prisonhouse is expressly designed by God to punish those who refused to be bound by His laws. In earthly prisons the poor captive has at least some liberty of movement, were it only within the four walls of his cell or in the gloomy yard of his prison. Not so in hell. There, by reason of the great number of the damned, the prisoners are heaped together in their awful prison, the walls of which are said to be four thousand miles thick; and the damned are so utterly bound and helpless that, as a blessed saint, Saint Anselm, writes in his book on similitudes, they are not even able to remove from the eye a worm that gnaws it.
>
> They lie in exterior darkness. For, remember, the fire of hell gives forth no light. As, at the command of God, the fire of the Babylonian furnace lost its heat but not its light so, at the command of God, the fire of hell, while retaining the intensity of its heat, burns eternally in darkness. It is a never-ending storm of darkness, dark flames and dark smoke of burning brimstone,

amid which the bodies are heaped one upon another without
even a glimpse of air. Of all the plagues with which the land of
the Pharaohs was smitten one plague alone, that of darkness,
was called horrible. What name, then, shall we give to the darkness of hell which is to last not for three days alone but for all
eternity?

Both paragraphs owe their intensity to the speaker's use of unifying
dominant impressions. The first paragraph develops the dominant
impression of the straitness—the narrowness—of hell; the second
paragraph focuses on the darkness of hell. No doubt hell is more
than simply strait and dark; the speaker says it's also noisy and
smelly. But he wisely refrains from trying to cover more than a single
characteristic of hell in each paragraph. Other paragraphs deal separately with the noise and smell of hell. The result is intense and con-
centrated description.

Beginning speakers often err in their descriptions by trying to do
too much at once. Impressions are jumbled in a hodge-podge mix-
ture of adjectives and adverbs. Sights and sounds are not sorted out
and developed in individual paragraphs but are, instead, blended
helter-skelter within a single passage. Such descriptions have no impact because they have no central theme. Better, instead, to select a
single dominant impression and to build a paragraph around it.
Descriptions, after all, cannot do everything, cannot include every
conceivable impression, cannot accommodate every sight, sound,
smell. Speakers and writers are therefore better off sacrificing com-
pleteness in order to achieve intensity.

In constructing descriptive oral paragraphs, you should avoid
using involved metaphors, complicated analogies, and exotic adjectives. Simple, easily understood metaphors can be used, along with
short, easily grasped analogies. The vast army of insipid adjectives—
nice, cute, pretty, sweet, awful—should be shunned. Each descriptive
oral paragraph should be constructed around a single dominant impression, which supporting details in the paragraph should then
develop.

The oral paragraph that divides and classifies

Imagine that you're giving an informative speech about poetry.
Somewhere in the speech you'll have to acquaint the audience with
the different kinds of poetry. You might use an oral paragraph, or a

series of oral paragraphs, to amplify and develop the following generalization:

> Poetry comes in four principal types: the epic, the lyric, the ballad, and the dramatic monologue.

Such a paragraph—having as its primary purpose the division of a whole into its constituent parts—is said to be based on the principle of division and classification. Entire speeches are sometimes based on such divisions. A speech on "Types of Life Insurance Policies," though intended to inform, would nevertheless be structured on the principle of division and classification. More commonly, division is used as the organizing principle in separate oral paragraphs. Here, for example, are three oral paragraphs based on division:

> There are five venereal diseases, all of which can cause death. Three of these have been eliminated by modern medicine, while the other two, syphilis and gonorrhea, are on the rise once more all over the world. Both of these diseases are mainly contracted through sexual relations. These germs spread to all parts of the body, and, therefore, anything the infected person uses is possibly an immediate carrier. These germs can spread to another human by an open cut if it comes in contact with the germs of an infected person.
>
> The symptoms of these diseases are usually disregarded by their victims. In infectious syphilis there are three definite stages, with a few weeks lapsing between the first two. This first stage consists of a hard chancre (SHANK-er) sore in the genital area. The second stage is a rash accompanied by headaches, fever, sore throat, or loss of hair. The third stage, after a seemingly dormant period of 10 to 25 years, makes its presence known by rendering its victim blind, crippled, insane, sterile, or dead.
>
> Unlike its counterpart, gonorrhea's latent stages are more easily noticed by its victims. The first symptom is usually a burning pain during urination. The remaining factors of this disease are similar to those of syphilis, and the results are equally as devastating.[3]

The first paragraph is based on a division of venereal diseases; the second, on a division of the stages of syphilis; the third, on a division of the stages of gonorrhea. Each paragraph is based on a single division, from which the speaker never wanders.

Some rhetoricians maintain that good speaking or writing is primarily the result of clear thinking. Nowhere does this notion apply better than to the oral paragraph that divides; for division is essentially an analytical act. And the commonest errors in division and classification are ordinarily based upon faulty thinking, where the division is either not derived from a single principle or is incomplete. As an example of the first of these two errors—where the division is not based on a single principle—consider this proposed division of poetry:

Types of poetry:
    I. The epic
    II. The lyric
    III. The ballad
    IV. Eighteenth-century poetry
    V. The dramatic monologue

Eighteenth-century poetry—the fourth entry—does not belong in a division based on formal types of poetry. The category of eighteenth-century poetry would be appropriate—along with Renaissance and Victorian poetry—if the division had been based on chronological periods. As it stands, the division is based on two principles and is highly confusing.

A second common error is when the division is incomplete.

Classification of students:
    I. Freshmen
    II. Sophomores
    III. Seniors
    IV. Graduates

Obviously, one important category is missing—Juniors. The error is glaringly evident here; in more complicated divisions, it would not be as obvious. Consider, for instance, this division of Samuel Johnson's works:

Samuel Johnson's works:
    I. His poetry
    II. His moral essays
    III. His literary criticism

Two important categories have been ommitted: Johnson's translations, for which he first became renowned, and his dictionary, for which he is perhaps best remembered. A lay audience would perhaps not catch the omission, but any Johnson buff immediately would.

Finally, there is the venial error in division, made when a speaker divides a subject into overlapping categories. Here is just such an error:

Kinds of love

    I. Romantic love
   II. Conjugal love
  III. Parental love
  IV. Christian love
   V. Erotic love
  VI. Love in an open marriage

"Erotic love" can, perhaps, stand as a separate category, but "Love in an open marriage" cannot, since it is a variant of "Conjugal love." Overlapping categories do no serious harm to the intellectual integrity of a speech, but they make speeches longwinded and boring.

In giving a speech to inform, it is highly probable that you will have to devise oral paragraphs that divide and classify. Common sense dictates that you do the following in such paragraphs. First, devote a separate paragraph to each division. Notice, for instance, that the paragraphs on page 181 deal separately with divisions of venereal diseases, stages of syphilis, and stages of gonorrhea. Second, make the division according to a single principle. If the principle does not yield enough applicable categories, find another principle to base the division on. Third, make the categories mutually exclusive. Check all divisions to be sure that you're not repeating information in one category that is already covered in another. Finally, make the division complete. An incomplete division may bamboozle some members of the audience but not all. In any case, the speech containing an incomplete division will misinform rather than inform about a subject.

The oral paragraph that compares and contrasts

A comparison attempts to find similarities between two subjects; a contrast attempts to find dissimilarities. Entire speeches are sometimes organized on this principle—of either comparing two things, contrasting them, or doing both in the same speech. Speeches that simultaneously compare and contrast two subjects are, in fact, commoner than speeches that exclusively do one or the other.

Consider, for instance, if you were giving a speech on this topic: "Hostel or Bed-and-Breakfast Lodging: Which Is Better for the Young American Traveling in Europe?" Implicit in this monster title is the intention of the speaker to compare the facilities of a bed-and-breakfast lodging with the facilities of a hostel. But it is nearly impossible to purely compare both, for items of contrast between them are bound to exist. The bread-and-breakfast lodging may be slightly more expensive than the hostel, but it is also likely to be more private and more convenient. Notice how naturally a comparison and contrast begins to evolve. The two topics go together as well as the proverbial horse and carriage.

But in separate oral paragraphs it is common to find either straight comparisons or straight contrasts. Here, for instance, is an oral paragraph that simply contrasts:

> Well, a just law is a law that squares with a moral law. It is a law that squares with that which is right, so that any law that uplifts human personality is a just law. Whereas that law which is out of harmony with the moral is a law which does not square with the moral law of the universe. It does not square with the law of God, so for that reason it is unjust and any law that degrades the human personality is an unjust law.[4]

And here is a paragraph that simply compares:

> Whales and human beings are like two nations of individuals who have certain characteristics in common. As mammals they both are warm-blooded, giving milk, and breathing air. As social creatures they both have basic urges for privacy as well as for fraternization. As species bent on reproduction they both show similar patterns of aggression during courtship, the male trying to get the female's attention and the female responding. Finally, as mystical beings they both are caught in the net of life and time, fellow prisoners of the splendor, travail, and secrets of earth.

Both the contrast and the comparison are done within single paragraphs. Items to be compared/contrasted are brought together within a single paragraph, and comparison/contrasting remarks made about them.

A comparison or contrast, however, may also be conducted over several paragraphs. Here is an example:

Our Puritan ancestors were preoccupied with sin. They were too preoccupied with it. They were hag-ridden and guilt-ridden and theirs was a repressed and neurotic society. But they had horse-power. They wrested livings from rocky land, built our earliest colleges, started our literature, caused our industrial revolution, and found time in between to fight the Indians, the French and the British, and to bawl for abolition, women suffrage and prison reform, and to experiment with graham crackers and bloomers. They were a tremendous people.

And for all their exaggerated attention to sin, their philosophy rested on a great granite rock. Man was the master of his soul. You didn't have to be bad. You could and should be better. And if you wanted to escape the eternal fires you'd damned well better be.

In recent years all this has changed in America. We have decided that sin is largely imaginary. We have become enamoured with "behavioristic psychology." This holds that man is a product of his heredity and his environment, and his behavior to a large degree is foreordained by both. He is either a product of a happy combination of genes and chromosomes or an unhappy combination. He moves in an environment that will tend to make him good or that will tend to make him evil. He is just a chip tossed helplessly by forces beyond his control and, therefore, not responsible.

Well, the theory that misbehavior can be cured by pulling down tenements and erecting in their places elaborate public housing is not holding water. The crime rates continue to rise along with our outlays for social services. We speak of underprivilege. Yet the young men who swagger up and down the streets, boldly flaunting their gang symbols on their black jackets, are far more blessed in creature comforts, opportunities for advancement, and freedom from drudgery than 90% of the children of the world. We have sown the dragon's teeth of pseudo-scientific sentimentality, and out of the ground has sprung the legion bearing switch-blade knives and bicycle chains.[5]

The first two paragraphs catalog the moral stance of the Puritans along with their accomplishments; the second two paragraphs contrast the morality and living conditions of modern America with the speaker's rather nostalgic view of the blessed Puritans. Though he argues somewhat glibly, the speaker nevertheless draws an effective contrast over several paragraphs.

The choice of whether a comparison/contrast should be done within or between paragraphs is generally dictated by how complex the comparison/contrast is to be and how complete. If it is to be long, complex, and detailed, obviously it should be done over several paragraphs. If the comparison/contrast is to be short and relatively simple, then a single paragraph will probably do. Efficient comparison/contrasts are rather simple to do. First, you bring together side-by-side the items to be compared. Next, you decide the bases on which you intend to compare them. Take, for example, the title of the speech given earlier, "Hostel or Bed-and-Breakfast Lodging: Which Is Better for the Young American Traveling in Europe?" In drawing up such a comparison/contrast, many teachers recommend that students simply make up two columns, one for the hostel, the other for the bed-and-breakfast lodging. The bases for the comparison are then listed in the margin and appropriate comparisons/contrasts entered under each column. Here is an example:

	Hostel	*Bed-and-Breakfast lodging*
1. *Expense:*	Hostel cheaper.	Bed-and-breakfast lodging is more expensive by about $2 to $3 per night.
2. *Sleeping accommodations:*	Guests sleep in a sex-segregated dorm.	Guests sleep in private rooms.
3. *Bathroom facilities:*	Guests share a common bathroom with others in the dorm.	Guests share a bath, usually with one or two other guests.
4. *Food:*	No food is provided. Food can be purchased, usually at a cafeteria.	A home cooked breakfast comes with the price of the room.
5. *Contact with locals:*	Contact usually restricted to other foreign travelers.	Host or hostess usually friendly and eager to talk about their country. Good means of making contact with locals.

In assembling this comparison/contrast, the speaker needs merely to elaborate on each point, and insert appropriate expressions indicating either comparison or contrast. The following expressions indicate comparison:

> also
> as well as
> bears resemblance to
> like
> likewise
> both . . . and
> in common with
> in like manner
> similar
> too

The following expressions indicate contrast:

> on the contrary
> on the one hand . . . on the other hand
> but
> otherwise
> however
> in contrast to
> in opposition to
> whereas
> still
> unlike
> yet
> although this may be true
> for all that

The comparison/contrast oral paragraph serves many functions in speeches to inform. Speakers construct such paragraphs to help them define, describe, or simply inform their audience about a thing by contrasting it to what it is not. In constructing such oral paragraphs, you should cover both sides of the issue and use appropriate expressions to indicate either comparison or contrast.

The process oral paragraph

Process oral paragraphs are usually spoken to answer the interrogative "how." A process involves a sequence, either of events or instructions. A paragraph that explains process might, therefore, give instructions on how to bake a cake, might explain steps one must take to get a bank mortgage, or might catalog the sequence of events that lead to botulism poisoning. In all cases the speaker is required to explain, in proper sequence, how a thing is done, or how an event takes place. Here is a process paragraph explaining how to sharpen a knife:

> The sharpening stone must be fixed in place on the table, so that it will not move around. You can do this by placing a piece of rubber inner tube or a thin piece of foam rubber under it. Or you can tack four strips of wood, if you have a rough worktable, to frame the stone and hold it in place. Put a generous puddle of oil in the stone—this will soon disappear into the surface of the new stone, and you will need to keep adding more oil. Press the knife blade flat against the stone in the puddle of oil, using your index finger. Whichever way the cutting edge of the knife faces is the side of the blade that should get a little more pressure. Move the blade around three or four times in a narrow oval about the size of your fingernail, going *counterclockwise* when the sharp edge is facing right. Now turn the blade over in the same spot on the stone, press hard, and move it around the small oval *clockwise,* with more pressure on the cutting edge that faces left. Repeat the ovals, flipping the blade over six or seven times, and applying lighter pressure to the blade the last two times.

The primary requirements of process oral paragraphs are clarity and a strict observance of proper sequence. Because sequence is more difficult to follow when heard than when read, speakers have to construct their process paragraphs with painstaking care. The process should be explained in minute, understandable steps. Process oral paragraphs should be as short as possible, and should use repetition and transitions to help the audience follow the explanations of the process. Such paragraphs should also be clarified and highlighted by gestures, diagrams, and emphatic delivery.

If the entire speech is organized around the explanation of a process, it is often useful to announce this purpose at the outset and to simultaneously divide the process into stages, which can then be used as headings for various paragraphs. For instance, if you were giving a speech on "How to Find a Job," you might word the central idea as a statement of purpose:

The purpose of this speech is to tell you how to find a job.

Then you can propose subdivisions of the process:

> Job-hunting, in fact, is easier if the applicant does the following: (1) finds the hidden job market; (2) locates the hidden job openings; and (3) sells himself to the appropriate executive in charge of hiring.

The process has been divided into manageable stages, which can then be treated separately in different paragraphs. Moreover, to help unify the speech, the speaker can remind the audience of these major stages just before amplifying on any one of them. For example, the lead-in to a new paragraph might remind the audience of the second stage in finding a job:

> The second step is locating the hidden job openings. How are these hidden job openings found?

Such repetition might strike the student as tedious, but it is necessary to make a process clear.

The oral paragraph that explains cause

Causal analysis—whether in a single paragraph or in an entire speech—aims at cataloging the causes of some event, or at documenting the results of some condition. Primarily, such an analysis attemps to answer the interrogative "why." "Why did the *Titanic* sink?" "What are the causes of backaches?" "What are the effects of inflation?" These and similar queries, when systematically answered in either a paragraph or a speech, result in a causal analysis.

Paragraphs structured to explain cause may either plainly announce that purpose or simply imply it. Here, for example is a paragraph in which the writer makes no bones about what he is about to do:

> Why have giants vanished from our midst? One must never neglect the role of accident in history; and accident no doubt plays a part here. But too many accidents of the same sort ceases to be wholly accidental. One must enquire further. Why should our age not only be without great men but even seem actively hostile to them? Surely one reason we have so few heroes now is precisely that we had so many a generation ago. Greatness is hard

> for common humanity to bear. As Emerson said, "Heroism means difficulty, postponement of praise, postponement of ease, introduction of the world into the private apartment, introduction of eternity into the hours measured by the sitting-room clock." A world of heroes keeps people from living their own lives.
> —Arthur M. Schlesinger, Jr., *The Decline of Heroes*

Plainly, the governing principle behind the structure of this paragraph is to explain cause—to answer its own question, "Why have giants vanished from our midst?" Once the question is answered, the paragraph comes to an end. Other business—further questions, answers, explanations—will be taken up in further paragraphs.

Other paragraphs that explain cause, however, may be more secretive about doing it—to the disadvantage of speaker, reader, and listener. Here, for instance, is a paragraph that attempts to explain the causes of air pollution, but in rather a roundabout way:

> Industry was once considered the major polluting influence of our atmosphere. This is no longer the case. The automobile has become overwhelmingly the most serious problem we face in air pollution control. As the Senate Subcommittee on Air and Water Pollution expresses it, "automotive exhaust is cited as responsible for some 50% of the national air pollution problem." And the problem of automotive fumes shows every sign of becoming more acute. While America currently has 86 million motor vehicles on its streets and highways, the Public Health Service estimates that we will have 120 million internal combustion machines on our highways by 1980.[6]

With some minor rewording, the purpose of this paragraph can be made plainer, and the material becomes easier to follow:

> Industry was once considered the chief cause of atmospheric pollution. But this is no longer the case. The primary cause of air pollution is, without question, the automobile. As the Senate Subcommittee . . .

All oral paragraphs, but especially oral paragraphs that attempt to explain so abstract a phenomenon as cause, are vulnerable to

Murphy's Law—"If anything can go wrong, it will." Indeed, had Murphy been a speaker, he might have coined a special law for the causal oral paragraph, "If anything can be misinterpreted, it will be." Speakers should therefore never try to disguise the organizing principle behind their oral paragraphs. If you intend to utter a paragraph that analyzes cause, no harm can come from announcing your intention. Endless misunderstanding, however, can result from your failure to do so.

Some paragraphs, instead of explaining cause, set out to document effect. For instance, a speaker may ask, "What are the effects of a progressive education?" The answer to such a question might result in the second of these two paragraphs:

> We are now at the end of the third decade of the national insanity known as "progressive education." This was the education where everybody passes, where the report cards were non-committal lest the failure be faced with the fact of his failure, where all moved at a snail pace like a transatlantic convoy so that the slowest need not be left behind, and all proceeded toward adulthood in the lockstep of "togetherness." Thus the competition that breeds excellence was to be sacrificed for the benefit of something called "life adjustment."
>
> With what results? We have watched juvenile delinquency climb steadily. We have produced tens of thousands of high school graduates who move their lips as they read and cannot write a coherent paragraph. While our Russian contemporaries, who were supposed to be dedicated to the mass man, have been busy constructing an elite, we have been engaged in the wholesale production of mediocrity. What a switch![7]

The first of these two paragraphs defines progressive education: the second analyzes its effects. If the speaker had asserted that students were delinquent and academically untrained, and then set out to explain why, he would have been analyzing cause.

Cause and effect are complex phenomena, and not easy subjects to speak about. Oral paragraphs analyzing cause must string together complicated propositions in sentences that are immediately understandable to an audience. This is exceedingly difficult to do and can result in an endless, longwinded speech. Moreover, causal analysis—whether in an oral paragraph or in an entire speech—is always liable to either logical breakdowns or oversimplification.

When delivering oral paragraphs that explain cause, you can take the following precautions against being illogical or being misunderstood. First, always use words and phrases that indicate clearly whether you are analyzing cause or deducing effect. If you are asserting one thing as the cause of another, say so. Use expressions such as "because of," "the reason for," "the cause is," that assert a causal connection. If you are deducing effect, you should likewise say so. Use expressions such as "the effect of this," "in consequence of," "as a result," all of which plainly establish the relationship of effect you are asserting between two propositions.

Second, if the phenomenon has several causes, beware of discussing them within a single paragraph. Cause is a complex enough relationship to explain in a speech. If you cram the explanations of several causes within a single paragraph, your audience will surely be baffled. It is better to enumerate each cause separately and to amplify each within different paragraphs. For an example of this, turn to Chapter 8, pages 117–18, where the speaker enumerates in separate paragraphs the reasons for the increased incidence of venereal disease.

Third, avoid the use of circular or ideological reasoning in assigning cause. Circular reasoning occurs when a proposition intending to assert cause simply repeats itself. For instance, the statement "Smog is caused by air pollution" is circular and silly, saying, in effect, that air pollution causes air pollution. Ideological reasoning results when speakers possess special beliefs that they are eager to assign as primary causes. For instance, the speaker who asserts that "The high divorce rate in America is caused by the unwillingness of people to be 'born again' " is guilty of ideological reasoning. Causes, like facts, should be nonsectarian, nondenominational, and neutral; any cause that requires the acceptance of some special ideological belief is immediately suspect.

Finally, in analyzing cause, you should always turn your attention to the proximate, rather than to the remote, causes. Some mystics and philosophers have insisted that everything is the cause of everything else. Insurance investigators, taking the opposite tack, distinguish between proximate and remote cause. Proximate cause is the cause most immediate to the event; remote cause is the cause most distant from it. For instance, a stockbroker involved in a car accident may have been distracted by recent reversals in the stock market; but the actual cause of the accident may have been brake failure. Reversals in the stock market and their effect on the stockbroker would therefore be a remote cause of the accident; the proximate cause would be brake failure.

Paragraphs of mixed purpose

Some paragraphs have one primary purpose—either to define, describe, or analyze cause—which they tenaciously carry out to the exclusion of everything else. The structure of such paragraphs is influenced by their purpose. Comparison/contrast paragraphs, on the one hand, will generally alternate back and forth between the items being compared, using expressions to indicate whether a contrast or comparison is being drawn. Defining paragraphs, on the other hand, will focus simply on saying what a thing is, either through the use of etymological histories, examples, or authority testimony. In either case, the primary purpose of the paragraph determines its structure. However, no rhetorician can classify or completely anticipate every conceivable paragraph structure. Language is too complex to be made completely subservient to rules. Effective paragraphs of a mixed purpose are written and uttered daily by inventive writers and speakers. Here is one such paragraph:

Definition: {

There are few words which are used more loosely than the word "Civilization." What does it mean? It means a society based upon the opinion of civilians. It means that violence, the rule of warriors and despotic chiefs, the conditions of camps and warfare, of riot and tyranny, give place to parliaments where laws are made and independent courts of justice in which over long periods those laws are maintained. That is Civilization—and in its soil grow continually freedom, comfort, and culture. When Civilization reigns in any country, a wider and less harassed life is afforded to the masses of the people. The traditions of the past are cherished, and the inheritance bequeathed to us by former wise or valiant men becomes a rich estate to be enjoyed and used by all.[8]

Analysis of Effect: {

We bring up the notion of mixed paragraphs to remind you, at the risk of saying the obvious, that language rules are made to be judiciously broken. Writers and speakers should not substitute the conventions of rhetoric for inventiveness. The point in speaking, after all, is to communicate, not to scrupulously practice a body of rules. Clarity and intelligibility should be the primary goals of your communication. The means by which you achieve these goals should be fashioned, not from the observance of rules, but from your own inventiveness.

CONSTRUCTING THE SPEECH TO INFORM

The speech to inform is made up of a multitude of paragraphs devoted to different purposes. In some informative speeches, especially one on a technical or abstract subject, it is necessary to begin by defining ambiguous words, phrases, and expressions. In some informative speeches, it is necessary to describe; in others, it is necessary to analyze cause and explain process. Common sense and the nature of your subject should determine exactly what kinds of oral paragraphs you use. Here, for example, is an informative speech on botulism. Like all speeches to inform, this one is made up of a variety of different paragraphs, each devoted to a different purpose. We have labeled the paragraphs to indicate the approximate purpose they serve in the speech. Intended as a model of the typical speech to inform, this example illustrates how a speaker fashions oral paragraphs into a cohesive, informative speech.

BOTULISM—THE DEADLIEST POISON IN THE WORLD

Opening paragraph uses anecdotes to arouse interest.

Central idea of speech:

1. The year is 1793; the place, Wildbad, Germany. Thirteen German peasants have just eaten a single sausage. Within hours, all are severely ill; within days, six are dead. The year is 1977; the place, Pontiac, Michigan. Diane Sprenger, a twenty-six-year-old nurse, has just eaten a mini-nacho, peppers and cheese on corn chips, at a Mexican restaurant. The next day, she is on a respirator, battling for her life. She is stricken with the same mysterious sickness that killed the six German peasants one-hundred-eighty-four years earlier. Its name is botulism, and it is the deadliest poison on earth.

Definition paragraph.

2. What is botulism? Botulism is poisoning caused by the toxin of the bacteria *clostridium botulinum.* *Clostridium* is Latin for "little spindle," which is what the bacterium looks like under a microscope; *botulinum* comes from "botulus," the Latin word for "sausage," the food in which the poison first

Student uses etymological explanation to help define botulism.

made its appearance. *Clostridium botulinum* is an ancient life form, billions of years old. It is an anaerobe, an organism that cannot survive in oxygen. The bacterium therefore lives deep in the soil, where air cannot penetrate. There, among the dark, airless, lightless dungeons of the soil, *clostridium botulinum* ekes out a meager existence by breaking down chemicals from the soil for its food. In such a state, it is harmless to humans. We often breathe it into our lungs with dust; sometimes we swallow it with our food. But it does us no harm.

Paragraphs 3, 4, and 5 have as their prime purpose an explanation of the process of botulism contamination. Notice how the student illustrates this process by the use of a hypothetical example.

3. But during times of drought, when the soil dries up and blows as dust, *clostridium botulinum* forms a shell around itself to shield it from the deadly effects of oxygen. This shell, called a pellicle, completely insulates the organism. Curled up inside its shell, in a state of microscopic hibernation, the bacterium is barely alive.

4. Then something happens. The bacterium, blown about with dust, lands on a green bean. The green bean is picked up by a housewife, who cans it. She boils the bean, and seals it in a jar. She thinks that by boiling, she has killed all the harmful bacteria. But she has not killed the *clostridium* bacterium. Because of its shielding pellicle, *clostridium* can withstand a half hour's boiling; it can survive freezing temperatures approaching absolute zero. The canned beans provide a perfect, oxygen-free environment for *clostridium*. Mysteriously, the organism knows when it is safe to come out. Dissolving its pellicle, the bacterium awakens from its death-like sleep.

5. Now it engages in a mysterious chemical process, something it doesn't do in the soil. It produces a toxin. The toxin is easily broken down by heat. Two minutes at 70°C destroys it. Even the actively living bacterium is now heat sensitive. Two minutes over the stove kills it. But if the beans are eaten cold, and the toxin ingested, the results are often lethal.

Mixed paragraph. Primary aim is to describe the toxicity of the *botulinum* poison. However, student uses a contrast to achieve this description.

6. How toxic is the botulism toxin? Toxicologists base toxicity on six commonly used measures such as a taste, a mouthful, an ounce. A poison is rated as super-toxic if a taste, less than seven drops or about 5 mg, can kill. Cyanide and strychnine are classified as super-toxic since 5 mg of either is lethal. In contrast, 0.00015 mg of the botulism toxin is lethal. The botulism toxin, in other words, is 34,000 times more deadly than cyanide. Isaac Asimov, the well-known science writer, says that less than an ounce of *clostridium botulinum,* properly distributed, could kill every man, woman, and child on the face of the earth.

Descriptive paragraph. Notice the dominant impression of botulism poisoning— "sudden, paralyzing, and difficult to diagnose." Details in the paragraph expand on this dominant impression.

7. The onset of botulism poisoning is sudden, paralyzing, and difficult to diagnose. Within six to ten hours after eating the beans, you have trouble focusing your eyes. The toxin has been absorbed into your bloodstream where it is now attacking your nerve endings, blocking the transmission of impulses from the brain. You can't focus your eyes because your eye muscles are becoming paralyzed. Soon you can't swallow; you can't move your limbs. Then the respiratory muscles go. Conscious but paralyzed, you slowly suffocate to death. If botulism is diagnosed before paralysis sets in, you have a chance of being treated with antitoxins. But botulism is usually not diagnosed. The physician will probably think that you have polio, myasthenia gravis, or hysterical paralysis, all of which botulism poisoning resembles. Once paralysis has set in, forget about the doctor. Call a priest. Within a day or two, you'll be dead.

Conclusion. What can be done about it? Student ends speech by coming back to central idea—that botulism is the deadliest poison on earth.

8. How can botulism be avoided? The commonest source of botulism poisoning is home-canned food. Before you can any food, get a pamphlet on canning from the Government Printing Office and follow its instructions to the letter. Cook the food in a pressure cooker. Cook at 124°C (248°F) in moist heat. Never eat any home-canned or home-preserved food unless you're absolutely certain that the food was properly processed. Only by taking the strictest precautions with home-processed food can you escape falling victim to botulism—the deadliest poison in the world.

NOTES

[1] Carl Rogers, "What We Know About Psychotherapy—Objectively and Subjectively," California Institute of Technology, Spring 1960.

[2] Ralph Zimmerman, "Mingled Blood," Interstate Oratorical Contest, 1955.

[3] Mary Katherine Wayman, "The Unmentionable Diseases," Indiana University, Bloomington, Indiana, Summer 1967.

[4] Martin Luther King, Jr., "Love, Law, and Civil Disobedience." Fellowship of the Concerned, November 1961.

[5] Jenkins Lloyd Jones, "Who Is Tampering with the Soul of America?" Inland Daily Press Association, Chicago, Illinois, 16 October 1961.

[6] Charles Schalliol, "The Strangler," Interstate Indiana Oratorical Association contest, Bloomington, Indiana, 1967.

[7] Jenkins Lloyd Jones, "Who Is Tampering with the Soul of America?"

[8] Winston Churchill, "Civilization," address as Chancellor to the University of Bristol, England, 2 July 1938.

CHAPTER

The speech to persuade

A companion's words of persuasion are effective.
　　　　　　　　　　　　　　　　　　　—Homer

WHAT MAKES A SPEECH PERSUASIVE?

A persuasive speech is a speech that tries to influence or change the beliefs of an audience. Generalizations about why such speeches are effective or ineffective are difficult to make. First, we do not completely understand how people think, form beliefs and attitudes, and we do not understand why they change them. Much of what is known about attitude change is theoretical and murky and varies dramatically from one school of thought to another. Second, a great deal of information about the most effective tactics of persuasion is contradictory. We know for certain that some speakers are more persuasive than others. But we do not completely understand why, and we cannot yet give a foolproof prescription for persuasiveness. The variables are simply too many.

But, obviously, some speakers are more persuasive than others—an observation virtually no one would dispute. Speakers are said to be credible, charismatic, dynamic—epithets that denote the willingness of an audience to accept their word at face value. Other speakers are regarded in exactly the opposite way, not meriting belief, approval, or attention. Why? What makes one speaker extremely believable and persuasive, and another dull and unconvincing?

Various answers have been suggested although none are definitive. Basically, however, an argument will persuade us for one of three reasons: (1) We are taken by the speaker's character, (2) We are impressed by the speaker's reasoning; (3) there is something in the argument for us.

The speaker's character

Consider, for instance, this situation. A single speech is tape recorded and played back to three groups of students. One group is told that the speech is by the Surgeon General of the United States; the second group, that it is by the Secretary General of the Communist Party in America; the third group, that it is by a university sophomore. The same speech was then rated by all three groups of students. The group who thought that they had been listening to the Surgeon General rated the speaker significantly more competent than did the other two groups. Moreover, subsequent tests showed that the group most decidedly influenced by the speech was the group that thought it had heard the Surgeon General.[1]

Since all three groups had heard the same speech, it follows that some factor other than the wording or reasoning of the speech was responsible for its differing effect. This factor was labeled *ethos* by the ancient Greeks, their word for "character." *Ethos* refers to the perceived character of a speaker, and especially to its effect upon an audience. Aristotle (384–322 B.C.)—considered one of the greatest writers on rhetoric of all time—made the following observation of a speaker's character:

> The character of the speaker is a cause of persuasion when the speech is so uttered as to make him worthy of belief; for as a rule we trust men of probity more, and more quickly, about things in general, while on points outside the realm of exact knowledge, where opinion is divided, we trust them absolutely.[2]

Further, he added that the character of a speaker is "the most potent of all the means to persuasion."[3] To put it another way, all other things being equal, we believe the speaker whom we think credible.

And where knowledge is inexact or controversial, we are especially inclined to follow the credible speaker.

Ethos, and its contribution to persuasion, has been much investigated, and Aristotle's speculations about its effects have been more or less confirmed. We are decidedly influenced by our impressions of a speaker's character. Studies have shown that children can be persuaded to eat less desirable foods because they are endorsed by a fictional hero; that students can be persuaded to accept false descriptions of their personalities when told that the descriptions came from experts; that, in general, people have a tendency to shift their opinions to make them conform to views attributed to prestige sources.[4] If you have ever wondered about the rationale for having football players endorse car rental agencies, or movie-stars rave about headache remedies, now you know.

The speaker's credibility

What factors give a speaker *ethos,* make a speaker credible? Isolated in various studies, three components of ethos have been identified: competence, trustworthiness, and dynamism. Audiences rating speakers as credible often attribute these characteristics to them. Competent speakers are characterized by audiences as being "trained, experienced, qualified, skilled, informed, authoritative, able, and intelligent."[5] Speakers rated as incompetent are ascribed the opposites of these qualities. Trustworthy speakers are rated as kind, congenial, friendly, forgiving, hospitable, and similar adjectives; dynamic speakers are described as frank, emphatic, bold, forceful, energetic, and active.[6] Audiences attribute the opposite of these cataloged adjectives to those speakers variously described as untrustworthy or undynamic.[7]

Ethos, in sum, is the audience's judgment of a speaker's character and credibility. Moreover, as might be expected, such judgments tend to vary with the topic. A speaker judged as expert on one topic is not necessarily judged as expert on another.[8] A doctor, for instance, might be rated as expert on a medical topic, but as unskilled on a topic of oceanography.

The speaker's values

Apart from the *ethos* factor, we are also more likely to be persuaded by a speaker whom we take to be one of us. This peculiarity in audience reaction is known as the "assimilation/contrast effect."

Basically, it says that audiences who perceive a speaker as possessing similar values to their own tend to exaggerate the similarity, while audiences who perceive a speaker as holding dissimilar values tend to exaggerate the dissimilarity.[9] The exaggeration helps the speaker's case in the first instance, but hinders it in the second. Salespeople, for instance, whether peddling cars, houses, or books, often try to insinuate similarities between them and their clients to take advantage of this effect. Here is an oral paragraph in which a speaker stresses his similarity with an audience:

> I must confess to a certain nostalgia on this great occasion. It was at this school over a generation ago that I had my first real contact with the world of ideas—with literature—with problem solving—with philosophic thought. It was here that I enjoyed close contact with a faculty which had some of the most competent, stimulating, and dedicated men it has ever been my privilege to know—men who have extended their own spiritual, intellectual, and moral heritage and influence far into posterity.[10]

ESTABLISHING THE SPEAKER'S ETHOS

What does all this mean to the student speaker? It means a great deal. Granted there are some elements of *ethos* that are fixed and cannot be manufactured no matter what the speech occasion. For instance, a student trying to persuade an audience to contribute funds for diabetes research cannot become a physician on the spot and therefore capitalize on the high *ethos* associated with such a prestige occupation. The status and prestige of a speaker cannot be altered for a speech, unless the speaker is willing to tell lies—which cannot be condoned. Yet the perceived competence of speakers also affects an audience's assessment of them, and it is possible for speakers to advertise their qualifications to an audience. Here is an oral paragraph in which a speaker tells an audience why he is qualified to talk about Malcolm X:

> I can remember a number of occasions when I talked to him, when I was with him, when I spoke on platforms with him; and

> so I am not indebted to printed material for my impressions of
> Malcolm X. I remember the last time he was in the city—not so
> much the speech, which was not one of his best by any means; it
> reflected, I think, much of the tension that he was under, much
> of the confusion, the constant living on the brink of violence. But
> I can remember him backstage, in the Gold Room I think they
> call it, of Ford Auditorium. Recently he had suffered smoke inha-
> lation, the doctor had given him an injection, he was trying to
> sleep, he was irritable. But he was here because he had prom-
> ised to be here, because he thought some people were con-
> cerned about what he had to say.[11]

Malcolm X had been dead for two years when this speech was given.
In this paragraph, the speaker is obviously trying to establish his
credibility by demonstrating, through detailed recollection, that he
was personally acquainted with Malcolm X.

Research on this sort of *ethos* building is contradictory and in-
definite. Generally speaking, however, excessive self-praise for the
purpose of building *ethos* can easily backfire and cause an audience
to feel disaffection for a speaker. But on some occasions, modest
claims by a speaker of personal experience or acquaintance with an
issue can certainly do no harm and might even do some good. For
example, in this speech, the speaker begins by identifying himself as
suffering from the disease he is about to discuss.

> I am a hemophiliac. To many of you, that word signifies little or
> nothing. A few may pause a moment and then remember that it
> has something to do with bleeding. Probably none of you can ap-
> preciate the gigantic impact of what those words mean to me.[12]

The speech ends climactically with an *ethos* appeal:

> I cannot change that part of my life which is past. I cannot
> change my hemophilia. Therefore, I must ask you to help those
> hemophiliacs that need help. For I remember too well my older
> brother Herbert, so shattered in adolescence by hemophilia that
> his tombstone reads like a blessing: "May 10, 1927–April 6, 1950,
> Thy Will Be Done." And I ask you to help hemophiliacs because

one day my grandson may need your blood. But I also ask you to recognize a hemophiliac for what he is today; to realize that past is prologue, that weaknesses sometimes begat strength; that man sometimes conquers. And so I pray: "God give me the courage to accept the things that I cannot change; the power to change the things which I can; and the wisdom to know the difference between the two."[13]

It is difficult to imagine a situation in which such an *ethos* appeal would not affect an audience.

The speaker's reasoning

We are also persuaded by the quality of a speaker's reasoning. Speakers who reason by documentation, support, and authority citation are more persuasive than speakers who merely generalize.[14] If you wish to persuade, you must therefore tell not just what you think, but also why you think it, and what evidence exists that supports your thinking.

Reasoning is an attempt to give logical and accurate descriptions of the things, events, ideas, and experiences that make up reality. None of us can ever be sure that our version of reality is exactly shared by anyone else. In communication with another person, however, we do our utmost to explain what we perceive and why we perceive it. We swap ideas and notions; we make assertions about the relationships between things, ideas, experiences, and events. We classify assertions as true or untrue.

To simplify such exchanges, logic was invented. Basically, logic provides us with a neutral and unbiased language for describing reality. The language of logic contains built-in safeguards against exaggeration and deceit; it is universal and works for all known conditions. The opposite of logic is mysticism, magic, or some other psychic manifestation. But the flaw of such systems is that they rely exclusively on the individual's personal and unique powers. Logic does not. Logical discourse is the most democratic of all human transactions. Logic asks only three things of a reasoner: clarity, consistency, and proof. The requirement of clarity means that all assertions about reality must be stated with precision. Consistency requires that logical transactions be impartial and unswerving. Proof insists that logical assertions about ideas, events, experiences, or things must be supported by evidence.

Essentially, a logical description of reality is one that makes an accurate assertion either that a proposition is true or false, or that certain relationships exist between ideas, things, events, and experiences. Here, for instance, is an oral paragraph that first makes an assertion and then proves it:

> Public ignorance is especially troublesome. Everyone generally feels that students who say they will commit suicide never do. This simply isn't true. Dr. Edwin S. Sheidman and Dr. Norman L. Farberow of the Los Angeles Suicide Prevention Center made a study of suicide cases. They discovered that 75% of these people had given clear and certain indication of their intentions, either by word or deed, before they finally did end their lives. One Yale student talked of being "so very tired of life"—then shot himself to death. Students who make such remarks must be taken seriously.[15]

This oral paragraph satisfies our criteria for logic. Its assertions are clear and understandable. The student does not garble or misstate her assertion about students who threaten suicide. Having deduced that students who threaten suicide must be taken seriously, the speaker—to observe the requirement of consistency—must not argue or maintain the contrary anywhere else in the speech. For an assertion that is true in one part of a speech is also true in its other parts. Logical truth does not vary with the phase of the moon, the position of the planets, or the gravitational pull of the earth. Such circumstances may affect mystical truth, but their effect on logical truth is nonexistent.

Finally, the assertion about students who commit suicide is supported by proof. One may argue that the proof is insufficient, that the study was not thorough, that more investigation is needed before the truth of the assertion can be accepted. Logical propositions are not immune from different interpretations. But at least the process and the proof by which the speaker reached her conclusions are perfectly clear. Reasonable people now have something specific to argue reasonably about.

Logical relationships

Other logical descriptions of reality assert relationships between events, ideas, experiences, and things. Such relationships are typically of cause, consequence, category, alternative, or analogy. In a relationship of cause, a speaker simply proclaims one event as the cause of another:

> Air pollution is <u>caused</u> by dirty emissions from the exhausts of automobile engines.

Assertions of consequence do just the opposite:

> Excessive spending by the Federal Government <u>results</u> in added inflation.

Assertions of category relationships simply classify one item under the category of another:

> The dinosaur's high metabolism and fast energy production <u>places</u> it not with the cold-blooded lizards but the warm-blooded mammals and birds.

Therefore, all that is known about the category of warm-blooded animals and birds applies as well to the dinosaur. Assertions of alternative do not classify but relate ideas in an either/or formula:

> <u>Either</u> we stop polluting the atmosphere with freon <u>or</u> we face the prospect of increasing cases of skin cancer.

Assertions of analogy simply propose a likeness between two ideas, deducing from the outcome of the one, the outcome of the other:

> The kingdom of heaven is <u>like to</u> a grain of mustard seed, which a man took, and sowed in his field: Which indeed is the least of all seeds; but when it is grown, it is the greatest among herbs, and becometh a tree, so that the birds of the air come and lodge in the branches thereof.

In other words, as the mustard seed fares and spreads, so does the kingdom of heaven. Here is another, more scientific, argument by analogy:

> Generally, palaeontologists have assumed that in the everyday details of life, dinosaurs were merely overgrown alligators or lizards. Crocodilians and lizards spend much of their time in inactivity, sunning themselves on a convenient rock or log, and, compared to modern mammals, most reptiles are slow and sluggish. Hence the usual re-

construction of a dinosaur such as *Brontosaurus* is as a mountain of scaly flesh which moved around only slowly and infrequently.

When attempts at logical argument fail, they generally do so for one of three reasons: They are unclear; they are inconsistent; they are unsupported. No effort will be made here to catalog every possible variation on these common errors. Unclear arguments, for instance, can be caused by any number of grammatical errors and oddities. Here is a proposition that is unclearly stated:

Poor: Studies show that the murder rates for police officers, guards, and private citizens are lower in states without the death penalty.

The implication of the assertion is that police officers, guards, and private citizens are doing the murdering. Moreover, the statement unnecessarily divides the population into three overlapping groups.

Better: Studies show that the murder rates are lower in states without the death penalty.

Link words

A chief cause of unclear assertions is the misuse of link words. Numerous words can be used to show the links between propositions, among them the following:

Link words that describe a relationship of cause

> the cause of
> because of
> is caused by
> is attributed to
> is brought about by
> is laid to

Link words that describe a relationship of consequence

> in consequence of
> therefore
> thus
> hence
> the result of
> is due to
> since

Link words that describe a relationship of category

> places it among
> belongs to
> can be classified under
> is a member of
> can be categorized with

Link words that describe a relationship of alternative

> either . . . or
> or

Link words that show a relationship of analogy

> is like
> can be compared to
> similarities exist between
> is analogous to

The list is by no means exhaustive, but these words are used most often by writers and speakers to describe relationships between ideas, events, experiences, and things. A common cause of muddled assertions is the misuse of link words. Here is an example:

> The theory of evolution is a complex idea wherein all living things are related to one another <u>since</u> they all come from the same common ancestor far back in geologic times. Through evolution, new species arise from preceding species of plants and animals that were simpler. This has been happening since plants and animals first existed on earth, and it is still going on. <u>Therefore</u>, all living things bear a relationship to one another and this is called the theory of evolution.

The link words are underlined. What muddles the assertion is the use of two link words, when one would have been quite enough. Here is an improvement on the assertion:

> The theory of evolution states that all living things are related through a common ancestor. New species of plants and animals are believed to have evolved from simpler species. Evolutionists contend that the process has always occurred and is still occurring, and that <u>consequently</u> all living things bear a relationship to each other.

It is now clear what two propositions are being described: the theory of evolution and its consequences.

Inconsistent arguments

Inconsistency is another flaw of many arguments. A common inconsistency occurs when a speaker asserts one event as true in one part of the speech and then assumes in another part that the same event is false. A second, and more complicated, kind of inconsistency can exist between word and deed. Take the case of capital punishment. A primary rationale for capital punishment is its supposed deterrence of crime. Potential criminals among us, frightened by the gruesome fate of other criminals, are supposed to be deterred from a life of crime. In the following passage, Albert Camus points out the inconsistency between this belief and the actual practice of executions:

> To begin with, society does not believe what it says. If it really believed what it says, it would exhibit the heads [of guillotined criminals]. Society would give executions the benefit of the publicity it now generally uses for national bond issues or new brands of drinks. But we know that executions in our country, instead of taking place publicly, are now perpetrated in prison courtyards before a limited number of specialists.[16]

This kind of inconsistency is not technically a logical flaw, since nowhere among the canons of logic does it say that people must practice what they preach. Nevertheless, an inconsistency of this kind—between word and deed—can cast suspicion upon the strength and sincerity of an argument.

Logical support

Finally, all logical relationships and propositions must be supportable. Some arguments are insupportable simply because they assert false relationships. Here are a few examples:

The shrieking of grasshoppers *causes* madness in infants.

One major *consequence* of smog is the glaucoma epidemic.

> Chickens are more closely *related* to fish than they are to ducks.

Other kinds of assertions are insupportable by their very nature:

> The bathtub is the most dangerous place in the world.
>
> Love is more passionate in the hearts of redheads.
>
> Americans are the most loyal citizens on earth.

None of these assertions are provable. Unlike these, the assertions made in a speech should be worded so as to be supported by evidence. For instance, although it would be impossible to prove that "the bathtub is the most dangerous place in the world," the same general idea, worded more temperately, could be logically argued:

> More accidents occur in the bathtub than in any other site in the home.

Evidence can be gathered and presented in support of such an assertion.

REASONING AND THE ORAL PARAGRAPH

The argumentative oral paragraph scarcely differs in structure from any other kind of oral paragraph. Basically, the speaker makes an assertion and then supports it with specific details. Here is an example:

> People can reduce and lose weight. Alfred Hitchcock went from 365 lbs. to a weight of 200 lbs. by eating only steak and cutting down on liquor; Jackie Gleason scaled down from 280 lbs. to 221 lbs. Maria Callas likewise went from a tumorous 215 lbs. to a trim 135 lbs. Even Lyndon Johnson, when he was vice president, lost 31 lbs. in less than 10 weeks after being elected to the post in 1961.

In support of the assertion that weight loss is possible, the speaker cites the examples of four well-known people who have lost considerable weight.

All the advice and prescriptions we have given earlier about paragraph building apply as well to oral paragraphs intended principally to persuade. If you intend to say that one thing is the cause of another, do so with clear and conspicuous link words. Paragraphs that make fuzzy assertions simply do not convince. Nor, for that matter, do paragraphs that merely generalize. Persuasive arguments consist primarily of specific assertions documented with a wealth of convincing evidence. You must not only tell an audience what you wish them to believe; you must also tell them why.

Appeals to self-interest

With the exception of saints, most of us operate on the principle of self-interest. Arguments are especially appealing to us when they contain some proposals to our obvious benefit. The worker is rare, indeed, who could be persuaded to refuse a wage increase on the grounds that the refusal would help stem inflation. Most of us simply do not live on such a lofty, selfless plane.

What are the needs of audiences, and how do speakers appeal to them? Various attempts have been made to describe the needs of people. One such description, by psychologist Abraham Maslow, classifies needs in a hierarchy:

1. *Physiological needs:* for the basics necessary to survive, such as food, drink, oxygen

2. *Safety needs:* for freedom from fear and harm, for security, protection, law, and structure

3. *Belongingness and love needs:* for love and affection, for a feeling of membership in a group

4. *Esteem needs:* for self-esteem, recognition, status, prestige

5. *Self-actualization needs:* for being true to one's self; for becoming what one is potentially able to become

The theory is that each level of need has to be satisfied before the desires of the next level are felt. For instance, we obviously need food and air before we can begin to fret about safety; likewise, we must be safe and sheltered before we can worry about belonging.

If Maslow is right, then it follows that various need levels exist at which a speaker might aim the appeals of a speech. These need levels will vary with the audience. A well-fed, affluent audience is not likely to be moved by a speech appealing to the physiological needs of hunger. On the other hand, a hungry, poverty-stricken audience is likely to turn a deaf ear to a speech whose appeals are aimed at self-actualization needs. Much demagoguery—mindless, stirring appeals—has been directed at basic needs. Potential dictators and political firebrands are generally more successful in stirring up the mob when physiological or safety needs are threatened. People do not riot because they have been denied a chance at self-actualization; they riot because they are hungry, or because their safety is threatened. Appeals to the basic needs are extremely powerful and rousing.

Motivational appeals

In the persuasive speech, some oral paragraphs are constructed to appeal to the level of needs that are important to an audience. Such appeals are a legitimate part of persuasion and are often used by speakers. Here is one such oral paragraph, whose appeal is to the "security need":

> What we must not ignore is the desperate urgency of the need for undertaking a new approach to the problem of people-to-people communication. Not only in our Cold War struggle with communism, but also in our relations with such old and close friends as France and Canada, it is evident that the rhetoric of international communication has proved inadequate to the demands made upon it. No one, I think, will deny that the survival of our civilization, if not of the human race itself, may depend upon the speedy development of effective means of bridging culture gaps.[17]

Various other appeals are possible. For instance, if you were giving a speech urging that the school bookstore be taken over by the student union, you could appeal to students' needs to economize. Motivational appeals are most effective when they go right to the heart of an audience's primary need. Before drafting such oral paragraphs, you should analyze the needs of your audience and try to devise the kind of appeal that is most likely to have a strong effect.

THE ETHICS OF PERSUASION

Ethics, like physics, has lately been dominated by relativity. Such an approach essentially proclaims that what is good for one goose is not necessarily good for another. Then there is the other ancient argument about means versus ends. Is it legitimate, for instance, for a speaker to use dishonest means to achieve honest ends? Or does the illegitimacy of the one taint the worthiness of the other? Such are the issues that theologians and moral philosophers puzzle over.

Our own concerns are more practical. We do not intend to discuss the borderline and knotty question of ethical behavior, but simply to outline, as clearly as we can, what constitutes an ethical argument, and what does not. To begin with, any argument that fails to focus on the issues is ethically illegitimate. Logicians have classified at length the various kinds of arguments that do not focus on arguable issues. Among these unfocused arguments are the following:

The ad hominem argument

Ad hominem is Latin for "against the man." Rather than arguing the issue, an *ad hominem* argument directs verbal vituperation against the arguer. Here is an example:

> My opponent, Mrs. Butler, favors the busing of children for the purposes of achieving racial integration. Naturally, she would take that stand. As everyone knows, she is what a former vice-president of the United States used to call a "radical liberal." She is pinker than rare roast beef. Nothing would make her—or Moscow—happier than the destruction of our neighborhood schools.

Such attacks, against an opponent rather than an opponent's logic, constitute an unethical argument.

The red-herring argument

The red-herring argument introduces a secondary, emotional issue that draws attention away from the real one. For instance, in an argument about whether or not schools should be allowed to lead children in group prayer, a speaker might say:

> The real question here is whether or not we intend to
> allow atheists to dictate school policy, whether or not we
> intend to allow atheists to run our lives for us.

That, of course, is not the question. Nor does it follow that an opponent of public school prayer is necessarily an atheist. Perhaps he or
she merely believes strongly in the constitutional separation of
church and state. But the assertion about atheists is so emotionally
loaded that it is apt to distract attention away from the real issue and
put opponents of school prayer on the defensive.

The circular argument

A circular argument is one that moves in circles. Here is an
example:

> We should stick to the spirit of the Constitution which
> requires us to preserve the balance of power between the
> different branches of government. And we should do that
> because the Constitution is the greatest document of gov-
> ernment ever conceived. And proof of how great the Con-
> stitution is can be found in its very sensible requirement
> that all the branches of the Federal government be kept
> separate but equal.

The argument goes nowhere and cites no proof. It merely repeats in
the second half what has already been asserted in the first.

The ad populum argument

The *ad populum* argument appeals to common feelings, pas-
sions, and prejudices through the selective use of unflattering phrases,
such as "creeping red socialism," "robber barons," or "demagogue
tendencies," to describe an issue to which one is opposed. Con-
versely, the favored issue is described in flattering terms, such as
"for our beloved country," "freedom of choice," and "good for the
general public."

> Proponents of the Panama Canal Treaty want us to take
> part in a "give-away" of American property. They want
> us to hand this tinhorn dictator over there some sovereign
> American soil. Why stop with Panama? Let's give away

Hawaii next! Rhode Island! Let's get in on the great
American give-away, the great American hand-out to the
freeloaders. But I say, I oppose this treaty because I love
my country, because you, along with me, are patriotic citizens, who draw the line at giving away even an inch of
American soil, soil stained with the blood of patriotic
Americans who went into that malaria-infested jungle and
built the canal.

Such arguments merely inflame the emotions; they do not discuss the
issues.

The ethical use of evidence

Used ethically, evidence is not distorted, exaggerated, or mis-
quoted. Speakers who are ethical will not use dated studies that have
been replaced by later ones, will not misrepresent the credentials of
an authority, and will not edit a testimonial to make it appear more
favorable than it really is. No great moral issues or philosophical ambiguities are involved here. The point is merely to play fair with the
audience, to share with them any reservations, conditions, stipula-
tions that accompany the evidence you use.

The ethical use of emotional arguments

Appeals that play on hate, prejudice, vengeance can never be
condoned. Such rousing appeals are the stock-in-trade of dema-
gogues and rabble rousers. But emotional appeals directed to our better selves and serving the cause of furthering an argument are
legitimate. Here is an emotional appeal used by the philosopher Albert Camus in speaking against capital punishment:

> Shortly before the war of 1914, an assassin whose crime was
> particularly repulsive (he had slaughtered a family of farmers,
> including the children) was condemned to death in Algiers. He
> was a farm worker who had killed in a sort of bloodthirsty frenzy
> but had aggravated his case by robbing his victims. The affair
> created a great stir. It was generally thought that decapitation
> was too mild a punishment for such a monster. This was the
> opinion, I have been told, of my father, who was especially

aroused by the murder of the children. One of the few things I know about him, in any case, is that he wanted to witness the execution, for the first time in his life. He got up in the dark to go to the place of execution at the other end of town amid a great crowd of people. What he saw that morning he never told anyone. My mother relates merely that he came rushing home, his face distorted, refused to talk, lay down for a moment on the bed, and suddenly began to vomit. He had just discovered the reality under the noble phrases with which it was masked. Instead of thinking of the slaughtered children, he could think of nothing but that quivering body that had just been dropped onto a board to have its head cut off.

Presumably that ritual act is horrible indeed if it manages to overcome the indignation of a simple, straightforward man and if a punishment he considered richly deserved had no other effect than to nauseate him. When the extreme penalty simply causes vomiting on the part of the respectable citizen it is supposed to protect, how can anyone maintain that it is likely, as it ought to be, to bring more peace and order into the community? Rather, it is obviously no less repulsive than the crime, and this new murder, far from making amends for the harm done to the social body, adds a new blot to the first one.[18]

Camus' use of emotional appeal is temperate and an integral part of his argument—namely, that capital punishment is immoral. Moreover, the emotional appeal is not used in place of logic, but merely as a supplement to it. In his talk, he goes on to argue logically against the efficacy of capital punishment. The ethical use of emotional appeal depends on the speech and on the speech occasion. Universal rules are difficult to make, but it is surely not unreasonable to expect that speakers will use their emotional appeals temperately, and that they will use them, not in place of, but as a supplement to, logical arguments.

I AM NOT THE CATHOLIC CANDIDATE FOR PRESIDENT

The following speech was given by John F. Kennedy to a special meeting of the Greater Houston Ministerial Association on September 12, 1960. Kennedy's purpose is to persuade the audience of ministers that his religious affiliation will make no difference to his being an effective President. During the 1960 campaign, the issue raised was whether or not a Catholic President, because of his religious beliefs, would be independent, or subservient to the spiritual leader of Catholics everywhere, the Pope.

Reverend Meza, Reverend Reck, I'm grateful for your generous invitation to speak my views.

While the so-called religious issue is necessarily and properly the chief topic here tonight, I want to emphasize from the outset that we have far more critical issues to face in the 1960 election; the spread of Communist influence, until it now festers 90 miles off the coast of Florida—the humiliating treatment of our President and Vice President by those who no longer respect our power—the hungry children I saw in West Virginia, the old people who cannot pay their doctor bills, the families forced to give up their farms—an America with too many slums, with too few schools, and too late to the moon and outer space.

These are the real issues which should decide this campaign. And they are not religious issues—for war and hunger and ignorance and despair know no religious barriers.

But because I am a Catholic, and no Catholic has ever been elected President, the real issues in this campaign have been obscured—perhaps deliberately, in some quarters less responsible than this. So it is apparently necessary for me to state once again—not what kind of church I believe in, for that should be important only to me—but what kind of America I believe in.

I believe in an America where the separation of church and state is absolute—where no Catholic prelate would tell the President (should he be Catholic) how to act, and no Protestant minister would tell his parishioners for whom to vote—where no church or church school is granted any public funds or political preference—and where no man is denied public office merely because his religion differs from the President who might appoint him or the people who might elect him.

I believe in an America that is officially neither Catholic, Protestant nor Jewish—where no public official either requests or accepts instructions on public policy from the Pope, the National Council of Churches or any other ecclesiastical source—where no religious body

seeks to impose its will directly or indirectly upon the general popu-
lace or the public acts of its officials—and where religious liberty is
so indivisible that an act against one church is treated as an act
against all.

For while this year it may be a Catholic against whom the finger
of suspicion is pointed, in other years it has been, and may someday
be again, a Jew—or a Quaker—or a Unitarian—or a Baptist. It was
Virginia's harassment of Baptist preachers, for example, that helped
lead to Jefferson's statute of religious freedom. Today I may be the
victim—but tomorrow it may be you—until the whole fabric of our
harmonious society is ripped at a time of great national peril.

Finally, I believe in an America where religious intolerance will
someday end—where all men and all churches are treated as equal—
where every man has the same right to attend or not attend the
church of his choice—where there is no Catholic vote, no anti-
Catholic vote, no bloc voting of any kind—and where Catholics,
Protestants and Jews, at both the lay and pastoral level, will refrain
from those attitudes of disdain and division which have so often
marred their works in the past, and promote instead the American
ideal of brotherhood.

That is the kind of America in which I believe. And it represents
the kind of Presidency in which I believe—a great office that must
neither be humbled by making it the instrument of any one religious
group nor tarnished by arbitrarily withholding its occupancy from
the members of any one religious group. I believe in a President
whose religious views are his own private affair, neither imposed by
him upon the Nation or imposed by the Nation upon him as a condition to holding that office.

I would not look with favor upon a President working to subvert the first amendment's guarantees of religious liberty. Nor would
our system of checks and balances permit him to do so—and neither
do I look with favor upon those who would work to subvert Article
VI of the Constitution by requiring a religious test—even by indirec-
tion—for it. If they disagree with that safeguard they should be out
openly working to repeal it.

I want a Chief Executive whose public acts are responsible to all
groups and obligated to none—who can attend any ceremony, service, or dinner his office may appropriately require of him—and
whose fulfillment of his Presidential oath is not limited or condi-
tioned by any religious oath, ritual, or obligation.

This is the kind of America I believe in—and this is the kind I
fought for in the South Pacific, and the kind my brother died for in
Europe. No one suggested then that we might have a "divided loy-
alty," that we did "not believe in liberty" or that we belonged to a

disloyal group that threatened the "freedoms for which our forefathers died."

And in fact this is the kind of America for which our forefathers died—when they fled here to escape religious test oaths that denied office to members of less favored churches—when they fought for the Constitution, the Bill of Rights, and the Virginia Statute of Religious Freedom—and when they fought at the shrine I visited today, the Alamo. For side by side with Bowie and Crockett died McCafferty and Bailey and Carey—but no one knows whether they were Catholics or not. For there was no religious test at the Alamo.

I ask you tonight to follow in that tradition—to judge me on the basis of my record of 14 years in Congress—on my declared stands against an Ambassador to the Vatican, against unconstitutional aid to parochial schools, and against any boycott of the public schools (which I have attended myself)—instead of judging me on the basis of these pamphlets and publications we all have seen that carefully select quotations out of context from the statements of Catholic church leaders, usually in other countries, frequently in other centuries, and always omitting, of course, the statement of the American Bishops in 1948 which strongly endorsed church-state separation, and which more nearly reflects the views of almost every American Catholic.

I do not consider these other quotations binding upon my public acts—why should you? But let me say, with respect to other countries, that I am wholly opposed to the state being used by any religious group, Catholic or Protestant, to compel, prohibit, or persecute the free exercise of any other religion. And I hope that you and I condemn with equal fervor those nations which deny their Presidency to Protestants and those which deny it to Catholics. And rather than cite the misdeeds of those who differ, I would cite the record of the Catholic Church in such nations as Ireland and France—and the independence of such statesmen as Adenauer and De Gaulle.

But let me stress again that these are my views—for, contrary to common newspaper usage, I am not the Catholic candidate for President. I am the Democratic Party's candidate for President who happens also to be a Catholic. I do not speak for my Church on public matters—and the Church does not speak for me.

Whatever issue may come before me as President—on birth control, divorce, censorship, gambling or any other subject—I will make my decision in accordance with these views, in accordance with what my conscience tells me to be the national interest, and without regard to outside religious pressures or dictates. And no power or threat of punishment could cause me to decide otherwise.

But if the time should ever come—and I do not concede any conflict to be even remotely possible—when my office would require me to either violate my conscience or violate the national interest, then I would resign the office; and I hope any conscientious public servant would do the same.

But I do not intend to apologize for these views to my critics of either Catholic or Protestant faith—nor do I intend to disavow either my views or my Church in order to win this election.

If I should lose on the real issues, I shall return to my seat in the Senate, satisfied that I had tried my best and was fairly judged. But if this election is decided on the basis that 40 million Americans lost their chance of being President on the day they were baptized, then it is the whole Nation that will be the loser, in the eyes of Catholics and non-Catholics around the world, in the eyes of history, and in the eyes of our own people.

But if, on the other hand, I should win the election, then I shall devote every effort of mind and spirit to fulfilling the oath of the Presidency—practically identical, I might add, to the oath I have taken for 14 years in the Congress. For, without reservation, I can "solemnly swear that I will faithfully execute the office of President of the United States, and will to the best of my ability preserve, protect, and defend the Constitution . . . so help me God."

NOTES

[1] Kenneth Anderson and Theodore Clevenger, Jr., "A Summary of Experimental Research in Ethos," *Speech Monographs,* 30, June 1963, pp. 62–63.

[2] *The Rhetoric of Aristotle,* trans. Lane Cooper (Englewood Cliffs, N.J.: Prentice-Hall, 1960), p. 8.

[3] *The Rhetoric of Aristotle,* p. 9.

[4] Anderson and Clevenger, p. 77.

[5] Erwin P. Bettinghaus, *Persuasive Communication* (New York: Holt, Rinehart & Winston, 1968), p. 106.

[6] Bettinghaus, p. 106.

[7] Bettinghaus, pp. 106–107.

[8] Bettinghaus, p. 108.

[9] Donovan J. Ochs and Ronald J. Burritt, "Perceptual Theory: Narrative Suasion of Lysias" in *Explorations in Rhetorical Criticism,* ed. G. P. Mohrmann, Charles J. Stewart, and Donovan J. Ochs (University Park, Pa.: The Pennsylvania State University Press, 1973), p. 62.

[10] Gerald J. Lynch, "The Pursuit of Security," University of Dayton, Dayton, Ohio, December 1963.

[11] Albert Cleage, "Myths About Malcolm X," speech given in Detroit, Michigan, 24 February 1967.

[12] Ralph Zimmerman, "Mingled Blood," Interstate Oratorical contest, 1955.

[13] Ralph Zimmerman, "Mingled Blood."

[14] Anderson and Clevenger, p. 71.

[15] Patricia Ann Hayes, "Madame Butterfly and the Collegian," Indiana Oratorical Association contest, Bloomington, Indiana, 1967.

[16] Albert Camus, "Reflections on the Guillotine," from a symposium with Arthur Koestler, Paris, France, 1957.

[17] Robert T. Oliver, "Culture and Communication," University of Denver, Denver, Colorado, 1963.

[18] Albert Camus, "Reflections on the Guillotine."

INDEX

Index